The Best of
Meer Taqi Meer

The Best of
Meer Taqi Meer

Selected Ghazals, Nazms and Rubaiyat
with their lyrical translation in
English and in Roman Script also

Kuldip Salil

rajpal

₹ 375
ISBN : 9788170289609
Edition : 2026

BEST OF MEER TAQI MEER (Poetry)
Selected and translated by Kuldip Salil
Printed at G.S. Offset, Delhi

RAJPAL & SONS
1590, Madarsa Road, Kashmere Gate, Delhi-110006
Phone : 011-23869812, 23865483, 23867791
e-mail : sales@rajpalpublishing.com
www.rajpalpublishing.com
www.facebook.com/rajpalandsons

Introduction

Meer Taqi Meer is the foundation on which the edifice of Urdu poetry stands. Building an edifice is difficult enough, but preparing the soil first and then putting up a structure on it is indeed the job of a pioneer. And as far as Urdu poetry is concerned, Meer is that pioneer.

Ghazal, as we know came from, and was perfected in Persian, a language which came to India along with the foreign invaders and rulers and held supreme sway at the Mughal court. It was also the language of the elite. Urdu was then at its nascent stage and was in the process of being refined. With the disintegration of the Mughal empire, however, Persian started losing its supremacy. It was being increasingly replaced by the language of the common people, which was Urdu, then called Rekhta. This language was assimilating and was getting enriched by regional languages like Brij, Hindi, Punjabi etc. It retained at the same time the sparkling quality of the Persian diction and its sweetness. This new language was fast gaining not only acceptability but also respectability. Wali Dakkani's Urdu Diwan was a landmark in this respect. However, it was Meer who perfected this language and made it a fit vehicle for Urdu ghazal as we find it today. It was his verses, as Meer himself says in his autobiography 'Zikr-e-Meer', (and not those of Wali) which became popular in the bazars and streets of Delhi. He created a medium of poetic expression which was acceptable both to the elite and commoners. Meer had a highly developed aesthetic sense and his language has the best of both the old and the upcoming. He was well versed in Persian and quite familiar with spoken Hindi.

Mushairas (public recitation of poetry) were popular in those days and the taste for poetry, unlike these days, was widespread. A good poet's reputation would rapidly spread beyond his circle of admirers and his city. It is said that Meer's poems were so popular that travellers from other parts of the country would carry them home. We have Meer's own testimony to it :

सर-सब्ज़ हिन्द में ही नहीं कुछ ये रेखता
है धूम मेरे शे'र की सारे दकन के बीच

My verses are popular not only in lush green (north) India
They have won acclaim in Deccan too.

A good poet in those days would not find it difficult to win the patronage of a nawab or a noble. This would relieve him from the drudgery of earning a livelihood and he could devote all his time to writing poetry. This is true not only of India of those days, in England too the poets lived off the bounty of their patrons and were known as 'gentlemen' poets.

Not only would a reputed poet not find it difficult to win favour with a patron, in fact a noble would welcome an opportunity of hosting a good poet. And this patronage would not make a poet at all subservient to his patron. Meer and Sauda furnish classic example of assertive independence, self-respect and outspokenness. Once the king asked Mohammad Rafi Sauda "How many poems can you write in a day?" "Three or four couplets" replied Sauda, "when the poetic impulse is on me; otherwise sitting in the toilet also I can rattle up three or four poems." "And these poems smell of toilet too." On another occasion, the king offered to make Sauda the poet laureate. Sauda rejected the offer then and there, saying "If I become the poet laureate it will be on the strength of my poetry." To Meer's notorious self-assertion and high brow attitude I will come later.

Meer was born in 1723 or 1724 in Agra. His ancestors had come to India from Hijaz, a place in Arab. They first arrived in Hyderabad, then moved to Ahmedabad and in Meer's grandfather's time ultimately settled in Agra which was then the capital of India. His grandfather served in the Mughal army. He had two sons. One of them was insane and died young. The other son married twice. From his second wife, he had two sons, Mohammad Taqi and Mohammad Razi. The first, Mohammad Taqi later came to be known as Meer Taqi Meer.

Meer was just ten years old when his father, who had turned a sufi and renounced the world, died. His stepbrother, Mohammad Hasan who was also his elder brother gobbled up all parental property and left it to Meer to repay their father's debts. All that the father had was three hundred books which the elder brother appropriated.

The repayment of debts was a formidable problem, and Meer was too self-respecting to ask anybody for help. But help came providentially. One of his father's friends, finding Meer in dire straits lent him five hundred rupees. Of this, Meer paid three hundred to the creditors, and leaving his younger brother behind, left for Delhi in search of some job. After wandering there for a few days Meer by accident met nawab Shams-ud-daula's nephew who presented him to the nawab who knew Meer's father. The nawab condoled his father's death and fixed a stipend of one rupee a day for Meer.

Ill luck was, however, pursuing Meer in Delhi too. The city was attacked and devastated by Nadir Shah and nawab Shams-ud-daula was killed. Meer returned to Agra where he was tormented by his relatives. This compelled him to head for Delhi again. He started living with his stepbrother's maternal uncle Khan Arzoo, who was a well-known poet of those days. But after some time, Khan Arzoo turned against him most probably because Meer's stepbrother poisoned his uncle's ear against Meer. According to some critics the reason why Khan Arzoo got annoyed with him was that Meer got emotionally entangled with his daughter.

Meer himself tells us the story of his tragic love affair. He fell in love with a girl when he was eighteen and she was sixteen years old and married. But the affair turned out to be failure because it would bring disgrace to both the families. As it happens in some areas even today in the twenty-first century, the families would take revenge on the lovers. Meer was persecuted so much that he went mad and was afraid of looking at the moon. This madness went on increasing. When all other medication failed, Meer's relatives tried the desperate remedy of bleeding him. And surprisingly, he was cured of his madness.

A big bulk of Meer's poetry laments the indifference and callousness of his beloved :

पत्ता-पत्ता बूटा-बूटा हाल हमारा जाने है
जाने-न-जाने गुल ही न जाने बाग़ तो सारा जाने है

Every plant and every petal my condition knows
Only the flower knows not, the entire garden knows.

Making no allowance for the social condition under which she lived, he continues :

मेहरो-वफ़ा-ओ-लुत्फ़ो-इनायत एक से वाकिफ़ इनमें नहीं
और तो सब कुछ तन्ज़ो-किनायत, रम्ज़ो-इशारा जाने है

Of courtesy, mercy, kindness, consistency, she knows not a thing
Too well she knows though satire and slant, sarcasm and fling.

And when he refers to shehr-e-husan (the city of the love) his accusing finger is turned towards the beloved :

चारागिरी-बीमारि-ए-दिल की रस्मे-शहर हुस्न नहीं
वरना दिलबर नादां भी इस दर्द का चारा जाने है

To cure somebody's heartache is perhaps not the custom
in this tinsel town of beauty
My callow beloved too otherwise surely knows the remedy

The fact of the matter however is that Meer's love was not only sincere but very intense; his passion for her was overwhelming. He was bewitched by her beauty and celebrated it in memorable verse :

जिस जा-ए-सरापा पे नज़र जाती है उसके
आता है मेरे जी में वहीं उम्र बसर कर दूं

Whichever part of her body I look at,
I feel like spending a whole life there

And this is not just adolescent love, it is an abiding passion. Meer is not the only one to be afflicted by it. We know how Ghalib fell for a dancing girl and wrote numerous verses on her cruelty, coquetry, callousness and worse. Outside of Urdu poetry, William Butler Yeats who is considered to be the greatest English poet of the twentieth century was clean bowled by the statuesque beauty of a nineteen year old girl, Maud Gonne. She refused to reciprocate his love, but he persisted and waited for her to oblige till the age of fifty-one, when ultimately he married. He so completely lost his sense of proportion that when Maud Gonne continued to refuse even after the death of her husband, he proposed to her stepdaughter. And coming back to Urdu, we have the famous love-tales of Majaaz and Sahir.

On the strength of his poetry, Meer found patrons in Delhi who held high positions in the imperial court. But the problem was that he would soon offend these patrons. Meer was highly sensitive, extremely egotistical, bitingly blunt, intolerant and at times, very annoying. The first among these patrons was an aristocrat Riyasat Khan, with whom Meer became quite thick but left him when Riyasat Khan asked Meer to teach a couple of his verses to a qawwal. Riyasat Khan had considerably relieved Meer of his misery. After that Meer got attached to Raja Jugal Kishore to correct his verses, but found little poetry in them and left him. He was given patronage successively by Raja Nagar Mal, Suraj Mal, Bahadur Singh Raza Khan and others. Emperor Alam Gir II also sent for him but Meer did not respond.

Meer's arrogance is well-known. When asked who are the poets of today, he replied, "First Sauda, next your servant" adding that Meer Dard is half a poet. At a mushaira in Delhi, he recited a masnavi (usually, a long love story) in which he described himself as a dragon and linked other poets to worms. At another mushaira in Lucknow, Jurrat, a well-known poet of the Lucknow school recited one of his compositions and received huge acclaim from the audience. But he wanted to hear a word of praise from Meer who sat quiet. When goaded repeatedly by Jurrat, Meer delivered a blistering reply, saying "You cannot write poetry; instead you should concentrate on your caressing and kissing." In Lucknow, even when Meer was dependant on nawab Asaf-ud-daulah for his very livelihood, he often came in clash with him. He would not even hand over a book lying near him to nawab when the nawab asked for it. He thought it would compromise his self-respect. He would point to a servant to do that. One day, when Meer was reciting his verses which the nawab had requested for, the latter kept playing with the fishes in the pond, Meer put the notebook in his pocket and came away. He took it as an insult and stopped going to the court. One day the nawab ran into him in the street and asked him the reason. Meer rudely replied that it was not good manners to hold such a discussion in the street. The nawab even then kept humouring him and sent a sum of one thousand rupees which Meer refused to accept saying that it should be given away in charity.

When Meer came to writing poetry, Delhi was in the grip of uncertainity, chaos and anarchy. After the death of Aurangzeb in 1707, Mughal empire was disintegrating. Delhi was being repeatedly invaded by Nadir Shah and Ahmed Shah Abdali. Rulers and emperors came and went in quick succession. Meer in his poetry, copiously lamented the plight of Delhi :

मीर तू बेचारा गदा
मिल गये ख़ाक में अफ़सर कितने

Lament not your lot O Meer, you are but a beggar
Many a noble has been ground to dust in Delhi

दिल्ली में आज भीख भी मिलती नहीं उन्हें
था कल तलक दिमाग़ जिन्हें ताजो-तख़्त का

They get not even alms in Delhi who till yesterday
Sat proud on the throne and wielded a sceptre.

It was under these circumstances that Meer received an invitation from nawab Asaf-ud-daulah of Lucknow. It could not have been more timely and Meer accepted the offer and left for Lucknow. The nawab received him with great warmth and took him under his patronage. Meer was relieved of financial worries, enjoyed some peace and security and earned much respect. The nawab would take him along when he went hunting. The result of these hunting expeditions were his 'Shikarnamas'. Also, it was in Lucknow that Meer wrote—'Zikre-Meer'—his autobiography in Persian. He was sixty then.

Meer was however soon disillusioned with Lucknow. In fact he felt ill at ease with the atmosphere in Lucknow which was full of levity, revelry, hedonism and superficial glitter. In poetry the emphasis was on formalism and sensual pleasure. It was a frivolous, light-hearted poetry in which wit, humour, banter and sarcasm abounded. There was no gravity and depth, only external brilliance was cultivated at the cost of simplicity and sincerity. Prosody ruled the roost and anybody who deviated was ridiculed and rejected. In fact Meer had a taste of this frivolous and shallow behaviour of the people soon after reaching Lucknow when he went to attend a mushaira in his old fashioned dress. The people there started sniggering, but when he recited :

क्या बूदो-वाश पूछो हो पूरब के साकिनों
हमको ग़रीब जानके हंस-हंस पुकार के
दिल्ली जो एक शहर था आलम में इन्तखाब
हम रहने वाले हैं उसी उजड़े दयार के

O you denizens of the east, you who find me poor
and shabby and laugh at me,
I have come from Delhi, the choicest of the world
once, but now in a shambles.

The people now knew who he was and apologized to him. In fact even when Meer was physically in Lucknow his heart was in Delhi :

खराबा दिल्ली का दो चन्द बेहतर लखनऊ से था
वहीं पर काश मर जाता...

How I wish I had died in Delhi for, even when in ruins, it was much better city.

Meer was a serious minded poet. He excels in writing about the gloom in Delhi, engendered by its devastation, its general sense of insecurity and sufferings of the people as also the rise and fall of dynasties. He is a poet of sadness:

दीदनी है शिकस्तगी दिल की
क्या इमारत ग़मों ने ढाई है

Of the sufferings of my heart, O ask not
What a structure have sorrows brought down

Or

अजब शहर था खयालों का
लूटा-मारा है हुस्न वालों का

What a wonderful city to think of,
Brought low by the beauteous folk.

In these verses, personal and general sorrows have mingled. His own deprivation finds an objective correlative, to use a phrase from TS Eliot, in the disintegration of the Mughal empire and general destruction including that of his house in Delhi. Add to this, the death of his near and dear, frustration in love, uncertainty of livelihood and a dark cast of his mind, aggravated by the treatment that he received from his relatives and his hyper-sensitive nature. Great poetry is often tragic poetry, for sufferings are eternal to human race, especially its sensitive members. "Happiness", as Thomas Hardy says "is an occasional episode in the general drama of pain". One reason why Meer, Ghalib and Zauq are great is because they enact before us this general drama of pain. Personal sufferings, when presented artistically and with intensity, become universal and find an echo in every heart. That is why our sweetest songs are those that tell of saddest thoughts. And in telling of saddest thoughts Meer has few equals.

In this respect, he may be compared with Ghalib :

कैदे-हयातो, बंदे ग़म असल में दोनों एक हैं
मौत से पहले आदमी ग़म से निजात पाये क्यों

Life's incarceration and bondage to suffering are the same thing indeed
Until our death, how can we from suffering be relieved.

Ghalib has, however, a sense of humour and can even laugh at his suffering, Meer lacked this quality. He cannot, for example, write like Ghalib:

कफ़स में रूदादे-चमन कहते न डर हमदम
गिरी है जिस पे कल बिजली वो मेरा आशियां क्यों है

Fear not and the garden's tale to me freely say
Why should it belong to me, the nest hit by the lightning yesterday.

Or

रंज से खूगर हुआ इनसां तो मिट जाता है रंज
मुश्किलें मुझ पर पड़ीं इतनी कि आसां हो गयीं

Once you get used to sorrow, sorrow it ceases to ebb
So many hardships befell me that they became easy.

However, if Meer lacks some of the redeeming features of Ghalib's poetry, he has the rare quality of illustrating and illuminating his observations from ordinary life:

शाम से ही बुझा-सा रहता है
दिल हुआ है चिराग़ मुफलिस का

As the evening approaches, my heart is in a state of gloom
it is like the poor man's lamp.

And Meer can also write :

शिकस्तो-फ़तह तो मुकद्दरों से है मीर
दिले-नातवां ने मुकाबला तो खूब किया

Victory and defeat depend on the fate O Meer
But my poor heart gave a good fight indeed.

Great poets create beauty out of sufferings, and, as in life so in poetry, suffering becomes a stepping stone for them to attain greater heights. And in the case of Ghalib, there was wine to beguile his grief which was not available to Meer. Ghalib could say if grief is abundant, so is wine. He was philosophically inclined, which Meer was not. Ghalib's poetry is a poetry of felt thought, whereas Meer is all feeling and less thought. Meer's poetry is turning loose of emotions, to use another phrase from TS Eliot. Notwithstanding all this criticism, however, it is a poetry of utmost sincerity and has a seal of authenticity about it. There is no artificiality which mars so much Urdu poetry.

Poetry works by suggestiveness and indirection, it is evocative. One of the many definitions of poetry is, what oft was thought but never so well expressed. Meer is not free from statement poetry, but in his best verses he enacts his ideas rather than merely state:

वो आये बज़्म में इतना तो मीर ने देखा
फिर इसके बाद चरागों में रोशनी न रही

She came to the assembly is all that Meer saw
But after that the lamps had no light left in them.

The reason why Meer's, as also Ghalib's poetry has a ring of sincerity about it is that they personally experienced what they wrote. It is poetry felt on pulse and oozing out from the heart. This lends intensity to Meer's poetry. It is poetry which has not only evocative imagery, but the imagery has freshness about it. There is aptness of expression and an insight into the fundamental issues of life. It was his search for poetic excellence, aided by his exceptional sensibility and understating of love and life, transitoriness of glory, wealth and greatness as also of vagaries of fortunes which was instrumental in pulling him out of insanity. Poetry serves as a therapy in his madness and he drowns himself in the task of perfecting his poetic craft, a task in which he comes out with flying colours :

नाज़ुकी उसके लब की क्या कहिये
पंखुड़ी इक गुलाब की-सी है

The freshness on her lips shows
A red petal in a red rose.

Or

मीर उन नीमबाज़ आंखों में
सारी मस्ती गुलाब की-सी है

Meer, those half-shut eyes surely link
With intoxication from alcoholic drink

And couplet like:

हस्ती अपनी हबाब की-सी है
ये नुमायश सराब की-सी है

Our life is but a bubble, nothing more
And the world is only a mirage at the core.

reminds one of the immortal lines from Shakespeare that life is a tale told by an idiot, full of sound and fury, signifying nothing.

Great poetry of human sufferings or tragic poetry even when it creates pity and pathos, is never depressing; in fact it is cathartic and illuminating. This is amply evident from the above verses. Poetry should give joy and strength even when it carries the full weight of our sufferings.

आग से आये गुज़र कर जल गये पांव तो क्या
दुख तो ये है वादियों में भी तपिश कुछ कम नहीं

We have walked through fire clouds, so what if our feet are burnt
But alas, in the cool valley also, we are burning no less.

and even in the midst of gloom:

हर पुरानी दास्तां से हमने पाया ये सलिल
ज़िंदगी तूफान है आदमी भी कम नहीं

All old legends bear testimony to it, Salil
That if life is a storm, man is quite a match for it.

It is this invincibility of human spirit which is celebrated in great tragic poetry of Shakespeare and the Greeks.

Though there is no general rule about it, it has been seen that many poets have done their best work in the first flush of imagination, that is in young age. It is true of Keats, Shelley, Byron, Wordsworth, Majaz Lukhnavi, Naresh Kumar Shaad, the great Punjabi poet Shiv Kumar Batalvi. (Firaq Gorakhpuri is a notable exception). The same may be said of Meer Taqi Meer. His best poetry, as critics have noted, is contained in the first two diwans. Meer's later poetry tends to be more a work of the brain rather than springing from the heart. It lacks spontaneity and looks mechanical and we have only conventional images and ideas strung together:

तेरी जुल्फे-सियाह की याद में आंसू टपकते हैं
अंधेरी रात है, बरसात है जुगनू टपकते हैं

Like glowworms flitting about in the dark rainy night
Remembering your dark tresses, I shed tears.

However, Meer's best poetry is truly of a first order; in fact, his highs are very high and his lows are very low. A poet is judged by his best and not by his quantity. It is not for nothing that Meer has won universal acclaim from succeeding generations of poets and readers. Acknowledging Meer's greatness Ghalib writes:

रेखते के तुम्हीं उस्ताद नहीं हो ग़ालिब
कहते हैं अगले ज़माने में कोई मीर भी था

There was, they say, in the olden days a certain Meer too
You are not the only master, O Ghalib, of poetry in Urdu.

Another contemporary of Ghalib, Ibrahim Mohammad Zauq, who was Ghalib's rival paid him rare compliment when he said:

न हुआ, न हुआ मीर का अंदाज़ नसीब
ज़ौक यारों ने बड़ा ज़ोर ग़ज़ल में मारा

Though many a one tried hard in the field of ghazal
None could attain the felicity that Meer had.

Towards the end of the nineteenth century, the prince among humourists and satirists Akbar Allahbadi wrote:

मैं हूं क्या चीज़ कि इस तर्ज़ पे जाऊं अकबर
नासिखो-ज़ौक भी चल न सके मीर के साथ

Akbar, I can never think of approaching Meer
Even Nasikh and Zauq could not measure up to him.

And in the twentieth century Maulana Hasrat Mohani compliments Meer when he says :

शे'र मेरे भी पुरदर्द लेकिन हसरत
मीर का शेवा-ए-गुफ़्तार कहां से लाऊं

My verses too are poignant, Hasrat
But how shall I acquire Meer's conversational charm.

Meer himself had written:

मुझको शायर न कहो मीर कि साहब मैंने
रंजो-ग़म जमा किये कितने तो दीवान किया

Call me not ye Meer a mere poet, Sir
My diwan is a compendium of sorrows and sufferings numberless.

Meer's poetry is a poetry of universal loss and sufferings, and hence its universal appeal. It is a poetry, in Wordsworth's words that sings of 'still sad music of humanity/ Not harsh nor grating but of ample power/ To chosen and subdue.' Meer's poetry outlived his times because he has the knack of conveying deeply felt experience and anguish.

As the noted critic Shamsur Rehman Farooqi says, Meer has written not verses but elegies of Delhi and of his own heart, and has lent a human touch to love and beauty. Meer has enlivened the sorrows of love and life. His poetry has obliterated the line between words and meanings and enshrined in it the development of Urdu language.

In Meer, the content finds its own expression and the two are fused. Since it is a spontaneous poetry, rhythm and melody come first and idea and thought later. He turns ethics into aesthetics, as Prof. Ish Kumar says. His poetry becomes a thing of beauty and a joy for ever. Addressing poets in his 'In Memory of WB Yeats' WH Auden writes :

With the forming of a verse
Make a vineyard of the curse
Sing of human unsuccess
In a rapture of distress.

Meer and Ghalib do something of this kind. Since they wrote on situations that we confront everyday and the dilemmas common to all of us, they cannot be dated. In the case of Meer, his use of the common man's language makes him quite accessible. It is poetry that comes straight from the heart and the impact is felt even before its full meaning is grasped. This is true of all good poetry.

As some writers on Meer have observed, no other Urdu poet has seen more ups and downs in life, none had to migrate so many times, had the company both of kings and mendicants received so much respect and seen so much poverty as Meer did. In Delhi Meer tells us that he had to go without food and had gone so weak that he walked from door to door taking the support of the connecting wall to ask for food. He had then to swallow even his pride.

Neither Ghalib, nor Iqbal, Faiz, Firaq and Ahmed Faraz - though all of them are great – will qualify to be called the poets' poet as Meer Taqi Meer will. He is not greater than all of them, but he is among the greatest. His poetry is certainly very uneven. A frugal critic has selected only seventy two couplets, from his six poetic collections or diwans which he describes as 'नश्तर' (rapiers).

He is a poets' poet in more than one respect. He not only chiselled the Urdu language and made it fit vehicle for poetic expressions but was the first to write so many ghazals which are not only good in themselves, but serve as a beacon for generations of poets, who borrowed heavily from them and acknowledge their debt. As Firaq Gorakhpuri proudly says about his own poetry:

इन ग़ज़लों के पर्दे में तो मीर की ग़ज़लें बोलें हैं

Meer's echoes are clearly audible in these ghazals.

Meer is quite conscious, at times very loudly conscious of his place in history:

पढ़ते फिरेंगे गलियों में इन रेख़तों को लोग
मुद्दत रहेंगी याद ये बातें हमारियां

People will go about reading these ghazals in the streets
For ages, what I have said will be remembered.

Even in Ghalib and Iqbal, Meer's echoes are heard loud and clear.

Meer's last days were particularly unhappy. For one, he was totally disillusioned with Lucknow:

मताए-हुनर मोड़कर ले चलो
बहुत लखनऊ में रहे, घर चलो

I should take back my wealth of poetry
For, I have lived too long in Lucknow and should head back home, (That is Delhi.)

His personal difficulties were piling up. In three successive years, he lost his son, daughter and wife. His health was deteriorating. Eyesight had become weak, and finally he was down with the painful disease of the bowels. And he felt quite lonely:

और कुछ मशगला नहीं है मीर
गाहे-गाहे ग़ज़ल-सराई है

I have no other hobby, Meer
Except occasionally writing a ghazal.

And even when he was universally respected, he died in 1810 at the age of 87 with a gnawing feeling that he had not got his due as a poet.

—Kuldip Salil

Contents

ग़ज़लें

Ghazals

ग़ज़लें

हस्ती अपनी हबाब[1] की सी है
यह नुमाइश सराब[2] की सी है

नाज़ुकी उसके लब की क्या कहिए
पंखड़ी इक गुलाब की सी है

मैं जो बोला कहा कि यह आवाज़
उसी ख़ानाखराब[3] की सी है

बार बार उसके दर प' जाता हूँ
हालत अब इज़्तिराब[4] की सी है

'मीर' उन नीमबाज़[5] आँखों में
सारी मस्ती शराब की सी है।

Hasti apni habab ki si hai
yeh numaish saraab ki si hai

Nazuki uske lab ki kya kahiye
pankhari ik gulab ki si hai

Main jo bola kaha ki yeh awaaz
usee khanakharab ki si hai

Baar-baar uske dar pe jaata hoon
halat ab iztiraab ki si hai

Meer un neembaaz aankhone mein
Sari masti sharaab ki si hai

---

1. बुलबुला 2. मृगतृष्णा 3. अभागा 4. व्याकुलता 5. अधखुली

Our life is but a bubble, nothing more
And this world, is only a mirage at the core

The softness on her lips shows
A red petal on a red rose

As I spoke, immediately said she
This voice must of that wretched man be

Again and again, to her doorstep I go
My mind is infatuated, or nearly so

Meer, these half shut eyes surely link
With intoxication from alcoholic drink.

मीर साहिब ज़माना नाज़ुक है
दोनों हाथों से थामिये दस्तार[1]

सहल-सी ज़िंदगी पे काम के तईं
अपने ऊपर न कीजिए दुश्वार[2]

चार दिन का है झमेला सब
सबसे रखिये सलूक ही नाचार[3]

जी में आवे जो कीजियो प्यारे
एक होवे न जो दर पे आज़ार[4]

हासिले-दो-जहाँ है एक हर्फ़
हो मेरी जां आगे तुम मुख्तार

Meer Sahib zamana nazuk hai
dono haathon se thamiye dastaar

Sahal-si zindagi pe kaam ke taein
apne ooper na kijiye dushwar

Char din ka hai jhamela sab
sabse rakhiye salook hi nachar

Ji mein aawe jo kijiyo pyare
ek howe na jo dar pe aazaar

Hasile-do-jahan hai ek hurph
ho meri jaan aage tum mukhtar

---

1. पगड़ी 2. कठिन 3. बेचारा (परंतु यहां इसका अर्थ है ठीक-ठीक) 4. कष्टकर

Times are critical, Meer Sahib, so beware
Save your self-respect with utmost care

Life can be a simple affair
Do not complicate it with needless bother and
useless care

Life has but a short span
Behave fairly with everybody, O man

Do whatever you like to do, my dear
But take care that your conscience is clear

What matter is how and what you say
Of course, you are free to say what you may.

होती है ग़रचे कहने से यारो, परायी बात
हमसे तो थमी न क्यूं मुंह पर आयी बात

कहते थे उससे मिलिये तो क्या-क्या न कहिये लेक[1]
वो आ गया तो सामने न उसके आयी बात

अब तो हुए हैं हम भी तेरे ढब से आशना[2]
वां तूने कुछ कहा तो इधर पायी हमने बात

ख़त लिखते-लिखते मीर ने दफ़तर किये रवां
इफ़रात-इश्तियाक[3] ने आखिर बढ़ायी बात

Hoti hai garche kehne se yaro, parayi baat
humse to thami na kyun munh per aayi baat

Kehte the usse miliye to kya-kya na kahiya lake
woh aa gaya to saamne na uske aayi baat

Ab to hue hain hum bhi tere dhab se aashna
waan tune kuchh kaha to idhar paayi hamne baat

Khat likhte-likhte Meer ne daftar kiye rawan
ifraate-ishtiyaak ne aakhir badhai baat

1. लेकिन 2. परिचित 3. प्रेम की अधिकता

Although by saying it one tends to give it away
What comes to my lips, I cannot help but say

When I meet him, all that is in my heart, I thought,
I would say
But as he came before me, the words could not find
their way

Now I too know your mind very well
The moment you say something, its drift I can tell

Meer has filled reams of paper as he went on writing
Excess of love has so much inflated his feeling.

दिल जो ज़ेरे-गुबार अक्सर था
कुछ मिज़ाज उन दिनों मुकद्दर था

सरसरी तुम जहान से गुज़रे
वरना हर जा जहाने दीगर था

बेरूख़ी का न कर गिला ग़ाफ़िल
रह तसल्ली कि यूं मुकद्दर था

आख़िरकार जब जहान से गया
हाथ खाली कफ़न से बाहर था

खुश रहा जब तलक रहा जीता
मीर मालूम है कलंदर था

Dil jo zere-gubaar aksar tha
kuchh mizaaj un dino mukaddar tha

Sarsari tum jahan se guzre
varna har jaa jahane digar tha

Berukhi ka na kar gila ghafil
reh tasalli ki yun mukaddar tha

Aakhikar jab jahan se gaya
haath khali kaphan se bahar tha

Khush raha jab talak raha jeeta
Meer maloom hai kalandar tha

My heart those days was grief-stricken
In fact, I was in a state of depression

You went through the world only casually
Otherwise at every step there was a new world to see

Do not lament your lot, you the ignorant one
Take it that your fate was thus written

When he left the world, ultimately
His empty hand stretching out of the coffin, one could see

As long as he lived, he lived happily and in contentment
Meer is known to have been a mendicant.

यारो, मुझे मुआफ़ रखो, मैं नशे में हूँ
अब दो तो जाम खाली ही दो मैं नशे में हूँ

एक-एक फरत दौर में यूं ही मुझे भी दो
जामे-शराब पुर न करो मैं नशे में हूँ

मस्ती है दरहमी है मेरी गुफ़्तगू के बीच
जो चाहो तुम भी कहो मैं नशे में हूँ

या हाथों-हाथ लो मुझे मानिंदे-जामे मय
या थोड़ी दूर साथ चलो मैं नशे में हूँ

भागी नमाजे-जुम्मा तो जाती नहीं है कुछ
चलता हूँ मैं भी टुक तो रहो, मैं नशे में हूँ

नाज़ुक-मिज़ाज आप क़यामत हैं मीर जी
ज्यों शीशा, मेरे मुँह न लगो, मैं नशे में हूँ

Yaro, mujhe muaph rakho, main nashe mein hoon
ab do to jaam khali hi do main nashe mein hoon

Ek-ek farat daur mein yun hi mujhe bhi do
jaame-sharab pur na karo main nashe mein hoon

Masti hai darhami hai meri guftgu ki beech
jo chaho tum bhi kaho main nashe mein hoon

Yaa haathon-hath lo mujhe maninde-jaame mae
yaa thori door saath chalo main nashe mein hoon

Bhagi namaze-jumma to jaati nahin hai kuchh
chalta hun main bhi tuk to raho main nashe mein hoon

Nazuk-mizaj aap qayamat hain Meer ji
jyon shisha, mere munh na lago, main nashe mein hoon

Forgive me my friends, for I am drunk
If you must, give me only an empty tumbler, for I am drunk

Just a sip for formality's sake in every round, you may
Fill not my glass pray, for I'm already drunk

My conversation may be meandering because of the heady drink
Say whatever you may, for I am drunk

Like a wine glass, hold me by your hand, or
Escort me part of the way, for I am drunk

Friday prayer is not going anywhere by any chance
I too am going, for a while stay, for I am drunk

You are too touchy Meerji, much like a brittle glass
Come not before me aye, for I am drunk.

कब मुसीबतज़दा-दिल माइले-आज़ार[1] न था
कौन-से दर्दों-सितम का ये तरफ़दार न था

आदिमे-खाकी[2] से आलम को जिला[3] है वरना
आइना था तो वले, काबिले-दीदार न था

धूप में जलती हैं गुरबते-वतनों[4] की लाशें
तेरे कूचे में, मगर साया-ए-दीवार न था

नर्मतर मोम से भी हम को कोई देती कज़ा
संग छाती का ये दिल हमें दरकार न था

रात हैरान हूँ कुछ चुप ही मुझे लग गयी 'मीर'
दर्दे-निहां[5] थे बहुत पर लबे-इज़हार न था

Kab musibatzada-dil maaile-aazaar na tha
kaun-se dardo-sitam ka ye tarafdar na tha

Aadime-khaki se aalam ko jila hai varna
aaina tha to vale, kaabile-didaar na tha

Dhoop mein jalti hain gurbate-vatno ki laashen
tere kooche mein, magar saya-e-diwar na tha

Narmtar mom se bhi hum ko koi deti kaza
sang chhati ka ye dil humein darkar na tha

Raat hairan hoon kuchh chup hi mujhe lag gayi Meer
darde-nihan the bahut per labe-izhaar na tha

---

1. मुसीबत सहने को तैयार 2. ख़ाक़ से बना आदमी 3. चमक 4. जिन्हें देश-निकाला मिला हो 5. छुपा हुआ

What misfortune was my heart not willing to bear
What pain and suffering was not in it already there

It is only this man of clay who lit up the world and made it look fair
It was not worth a gaze earlier though the mirror was already there

The corpses of the poor exiles burnt in the blazing sun
But in your street there was not a wall to provide shade to anyone

I would not mind O death if I were given a heart softer than the wax too
But that which lies like a stone in the breast would not do

Last night O Meer, I went suddenly quiet
My heart was home to many a sorrow but my lips were sealed tight.

झुमकी[1] दिखा के तूर[2] को जिन ने जला दिया
आई क़यामत उस ने जो पर्दा उठा दिया

उस फ़ितने[3] को जगा के पशेमां हुई[4] नसीम
क्या-क्या अज़ीज़ लोगों को उसने सुला दिया

अब भी दिमाग़े-रफ़ता[5] हमारा है अर्श पर
गो आसमां ने ख़ाक़ में हमको मिला दिया

क्या-क्या ज़यान[6] मीर ने खींचे हैं इश्क़ में
दिल हाथ से दिया है जुदा, सर जुदा दिया

Jhumki dikha ke toor ko jin ne jala diya
aayi quamat un ne jo parda utha diya

Us phitne ko jaga ke pasheman hui Naseem
kya-kya azeez logon ko unne sula diya

Ab bhi dimage-rafta humara hai arsh per
go aasmaan ne khaaq mein humko mila diya

Kya-kya zayaan Meer ne khinche hain ishq mein
dil haath se diya hai juda, sar juda diya

---

1. एक झलक 2. पहाड़ का नाम 3. बला 4. पछताई 5. अतीत 6. नुकसान, मुसीबतें

One glimpse from Him and Mount Sinai was all a flame
Doom descended on earth whenever unveiled He came

The breeze regrets having woken up this terror
To eternal sleep has it sent the people who were the world's wonder

Although heavens have grounded us to dust already
Our swollen heads are puffed up still with past glory

What sufferings in love Meer has not gone through
He first gave his head and then lost his heart too.

जिस सर को ग़रूर आज है यों ताजवरी का
कल उस प' यही शोर है फिर नौहागरी[1] का

आफ़ाक[2] की मंज़िल से गया कौन सलामत
असबाब लुटा राह में याँ हर सफ़री का

ज़िंदाँ में भी शोरिश[3] न गई अपने जुनूँ की
अब संग मदावा है[4] इस आशुफ्तासरी[5] का

ले साँस भी आहिस्ता कि नाजुक है बहुत काम
आफ़ाक की इस कारगह-ए-शीशागरी[6] का

Jis sar ko gharoor aaj hai yon taajvari ka
Kal us pe yahi shor hai phir nauhagri ka

Aaphaak ki manzil se gaya kaun salamat
asbaab luta raah mein yaan har safri ka

Jindan mein bhi shorish na gayi apne junoon ki
ab sang madava hai is aashuftasari ka

Le saans bhi aahista ki nazuk hai bahut kaam
aaphaak ki is kaargah-e-shishagari ka

1. विलाप 2. संसार 3. उन्माद 4. पत्थर ही इलाज है 5. पागलपन 6. काँच का सामान बनाने का काम।

The head that so proudly wears the crown today
Tomorrow, the cries of mourning will cover it all the way

No one has gone from this world sound and square
Every traveller who came, lost his belongings here

Even in prison, my passion lost not its intensity
For this mad head of mine, only the stone can a cure be

So delicate is the workmanship of this world's glass factory
That even your breathing here should most gentle be.

जो इस शोर से 'मीर' रोता रहेगा
तो हमसाया काहे को सोता रहेगा

मुझे काम रोने से अक्सर है नासेह[1]
तू कब तक मिरे मुँह को धोता रहेगा

मिरे दिल ने वो नाला पैदा किया है
जरस[2] के भी जो होश खोता रहेगा

मैं वो रोने वाला चला हूँ जहाँ से
जिसे अब्र हर साल रोता रहेगा

बस ऐ 'मीर' मिज़गा[3] से पोंछ आँसुओं को
तू कब तक ये मोती पिरोता रहेगा

Jo is shor se 'Meer' rota rahega
to humsaya kaahe ko sota rahega

Mujhe kaam rone se aksar hai naaseh
tu kab tak mire munh ko dhota rahega

Mire dil ne who naala paida kiya hai
jaras ke bhi jo hosh khoto rahega

Main woh rone wala chala hoon jahaan se
jise abra har saal rota rahega

Bus ae 'Meer' mizga se ponchh aansunon ko
tu kab tak ye moti pirota rahega

---

1. उपदेशक 2. घंटा, घड़ियाल 3. पलक।

If Meer continues so loudly to weep
How can his neighbour possibly sleep?

How long will you go on washing my face?
O preacher, I am given to weeping in any case

My heart has given out such a cry
That heaven itself will be puzzled by

I am leaving this world now, but I have been such
a mourner deep
That the clouds will, every year, for me weep

Enough, O Meer, now wipe your tear
How long will you go on weeping, my dear.

उलटी हो गईं सब तदबीरें कुछ न दवा ने काम किया
देखा! इस बीमारि-ए-दिल ने आखिर काम तमाम किया

अहद-ए-जवानी रो-रो काटा, पीरी में ली आँखें मूँद
यानी रात बहुत थे जागे, सुबह हुई आराम किया

नाहक़ हम मजबूरों पर यह तोहमत है मुख्तारी की
चाहते हैं सो आप करे हैं हमको अबस[1] बदनाम किया

याँ के सपैद-ओ-सियह में हमको दख़्ल जो है सो इतना है
रात को रो-रो सुबह किया या दिन को जूँ तू शाम किया

मीर के दीनो-मज़हब को अब पूछो क्या हो उसने तो
क़श्क़ा[2] खैंचा, दहर[3] में बैठा, कब का तर्क-इस्लाम किया

Ulati ho gayin sab tadbirein kuchh na dava na kaam kiya
dekha! is bimari-e-dil ne aakhir kaam tamaam kiya

Ahad-e-jawani ro-ro kaata, peeri mein li aankhen moond
yaani raat bahut the jaage, subah hui araam kiya

Naahaq hum majburon per yeh tohmat hai mukhtari ki
chahte hain so aap kare hain humko abas badnaam kiya

Yaan ke sapaid-o-siyeh mein humko dakhal jo hai so itna hai
raat ko ro-ro subah kiya ya din ko joon toon shaam kiya

Meer ke dino-mazhab ko ab puchho kya ho unne to
kashka khaincha dehr mein baitha, kab ka tark-islaam kiya

---

1. व्यर्थ 2. तिलक 3. मंदिर

All our efforts went unavailing, the medicine could
no relief bring
This heart-ailment, you can see, has ultimately ended
everything

All my youth, I cried and cried, and in old age closed
my eyes
I keep awake all night, so to say, and sleep when
the dawn arrives

Without rhyme or reason, I, the helpless one, am
credited with supremacy
He has his way in everything and blames me
unnecessarily

All the power, I have in the affairs here, is only this
much, indeed
I cry all night till the morning, and see the morning
somehow into the evening lead

About Meer's faith and religion, you that would like
to know
He sits in the temple with vermilion on his forehead,
he gave up Islam long ago.

पत्ता-पत्ता बूटा-बूटा हाल हमारा जाने है
जाने न जाने गुल ही न जाने बाग़ तो सारा जाने है

चारागरी[1] बीमारि-ए-दिल की रस्म-ए-शहर-ए-हुस्न[2] नहीं
वरना दिलबर नादाँ भी इस दर्द का चारा जाने है

मेहर-ओ-वफा-ओ-लुत्फ़-ओ-इनायत[3] एक से वाक़िफ़ इनमें नहीं
और तो सब कुछ तन्ज़-ओ-किनारा[4], रम्ज़-ओ-इशारा जाने है

क्या क्या फ़ितने[5] सर पर उसके लाता है माशूक़ अपना
जिस बेदिल, बेताब-ओ-तब[6] को इश्क का मारा जाने है

आशिक़-सा तो सादा कोई और न होगा दुनिया में
जी के ज़ियाँ को इश्क़ में उसके अपने वारां जाने है

Patta-patta buta-buta haal humara jaane hai
jaane na jaane gul hi na jaane baagh to saara jaane hai

Charagari bimari-e-dil ki rasm-e-shehar-e-husn nahin
varna dilbar nadaan bhi is dard ka chara jaane hai

Mehr-o-wafa-o-lutf-o-inayat ek se vakif inmein nahin
aur to sub kuchh-tanz-o-kinara, ramz-o-ishara jaane hai

Kya kya phitne sar per uske laata hai mashooq apna
jis bedil, betaab-o-tab ko ishq ka maara jaane hai

Aashiq-sa to saada koi aur na hoga duniya mein
ji ke jiyaan ko ishq mein uske apne varaan jaane hai

---

1. इलाज 2. शहर के हसीनों की परंपरा 3. कृपा, अनुकंपा 4. व्यंग्य, संकेत 5. उपद्रव 6. कटुता सहने वाला।

Every plant and every petal my condition knows
Only the flower knows not, the entire garden knows

To cure somebody's heartache is perhaps not the custom in this tinsel town of beauty
My callow beloved too otherwise knows the cure of it surely

Of courtesy, mercy, kindness, consistency—she knows nothing
Too well she knows satire and slant, sarcasm and fling

Only a lovelorn feeble man knows how much heartlessness can sting
And what troubles the beloved on one's head doth bring

Nobody in the world can be as simple as a lover
When in love, his heart's enemy, his god does he consider.

हमारे आगे तेरा जब कसू ने नाम लिया
दिले-सितमज़दा[1] को हमनें थाम-थाम लिया

कसम जो खाइए तो ताला-ए-जुलेखा[2] की
अज़ीज़े मिस्र को भी साहिब इक गुलाम किया

खराब रहते थे मस्जिद के आगे मैखाने
निगाहे-मस्त ने साकी की इन्तकाम[3] लिया

मेरे सलीके से मेरी निभी मुहब्बत में
तमाम उम्र नाकामियों से काम लिया

अगरचे गोशां-गज़ीं[4] हूँ शायरों में मीर
प[5] मेरे शोर ने रुए-ज़मीं तमाम लिया

Hamare aage tera jab Kasu ne nam liya
dile-sitamzada ko humne thaam-thaam liya

Kasam jo khaiye to tala-e-zulekha ki
azize Misra ko bhi sahib ik gulam kiya

Kharab rehte the masjid ke aage maikhane
nigahe-mast ne saaqi ki intkaam liya

Mere salike se meri nibhi muhabbat mein
tamaam umre nakamiyon se kaam liya

Agarache goshan-gazhi hoon shayaron mein Meer
pe mere shor ne rue-zamin tamaam liya

---

1. सितम का मारा हुआ 2. दुष्ट जुलेखा 3. बदला 4. संकोची 5. लेकिन

Whenever somebody before me mentioned your
name
I alone know with what difficulty under my control
my stricken heart came

Swear by Zulekha, the wicked, if you must swear
She enslaved the person whom all of Egypt held
most dear

In front of the mosque the tavern looked
but slight
Intoxicating eye of the saqi took its revenge right

I could sustain myself in love only because of my
conduct and grace
All my life otherwise, I had only failures to face

Although I fight shy of name and fame
My poetry Meer, commands worldwide acclaim.

इब्तदा-ए-इश्क़ है रोता है क्या
आगे-आगे देखिए होता है क्या

काफ़ले में सुबह के इक शोर है
यानि, ग़ाफिल, हम चले सोता है क्या

सब्ज़ होती ही नहीं ये सरज़मीं
तुख्मे-ख्वाहिश[1] दिल में तू बोता है क्या

ये निशाने-इश्क़ हैं, जाते नहीं
दाग़ छाती के इबस[2] धोता है क्या

ग़ैरते-यूसफ़[3] है ये वक़्ते-अज़ीज़
मीर इसको रायगां[4] खोता है क्या

Ibtada-e-ishq hai rota hai kya
aage-aage dekhiye hota hai kya

Kaafle mein subah ke ik shor hai
yaani, gaphil, hum chale sota hai kya

Sabz hoti hi nahin ye sarzamin
tukhme-khwahish dil mein tu bota hai kya

Ye nishane-ishq hain, jaate nahin
daagh chhati ke ibus dhota hai kya

Ghairate-yusaf hai ye vakte-azeez
Meer isko rayegan khota hai kya

---

1. इच्छा का पौधा 2. बेकार, फज़ूल 3. यूसफ से बढ़कर 4. बेकार

It is only the beginning of love and you are beginning
to cry
You know not as yet the hazards that on this path lie

The morning's caravan is up and about already,
Warning that it is leaving while you still lie lazily

Never will any greenery on this soil grow
What for the seeds of desire in your heart you sow

Hard as you try to wash them though
These scars of love will never go

More precious than legendry Yusuf, O Meer, time
is money
Be mindful, don't waste it, honey.

मेहर की तुझसे तवक्को[1] थी सितमगर निकला
मोम समझे थे तेरे दिल को सो पत्थर निकला

दिल की आबादी की इस हद है ख़राबी कि न पूछ
जाना जाता है कि इस राह से लश्कर निकला

अश्क़े-तर, क़तरा-ए-खूं, लख्ते-जिगर[2], यारा-ए-दिल
एक से एक अदद आँख से बेहतर निकला

दाग़ हूँ रश्के-मुहब्बत[3] से कि इतना बेताब
किस की तस्कीं[4] के लिये घर से तू बाहर निकला

हमने जाना था लिखेगा तू कोई हर्फ़, ऐ मीर
पर तेरा नामा तो शौक का इक दफ़तर निकला

Mehar ki tujhse tavakko thi sitamgar nikla
mom samjhe the tere dil ko so pathar nikla

Dil ki aabadi ki is hud hai kharabi ki na puchh
jaana jaata hai ki is raah se lashkar nikla

Ashqe-tar, qatara-e-khoon, lakhte-jigar, yaara-e-dil
ek se ek adad aankh se behtar nikla

Daagh hoon rashke-muhabbat se ke itna betaab
kis ki taskin ke liye ghar se tu baahar nikla

Humne jaana tha likhega tu koi hurf, ae Meer
per tera naama to shauk ka ik daftar nikla

---

1. अपेक्षा 2. जिगर का टुकड़ा 3. प्यार में ईर्ष्या 4. सांत्वना

We expected kindness from you, but you are callous
and cruelty-prone
We hoped that you had a heart, soft like wax but
it turns out to be a stone

My heart is so thoroughly devastated that it's better
nothing to say
It appears that a marauding army has passed this way

A drop of my blood, a portion of my heart and what
else not is my trickling tear
And each one of these foes of mine is more precious
than its predecessor

I am burning with jealousy in love and am keen to
know for whose sake
Out of your house this foray you make

We thought you would write a brief note O Meer,
to be easily read
But you have penned a whole discourse on love,
instead.

ग़म रहा जब तक कि दम में दम रहा
दिल के जाने का निहायत ग़म रहा

ज़ुल्फें खोले तू तो टुक आया नज़र
उम्र भर यां कामे-दिल बरहम[1] रहा

उसके लब से तल्ख़[2] हम सुनते रहे
मेरे हक में आबे-हेवां[3] सम[4] रहा

मेरे रोने की हक़ीक़त जिसमें थी
एक मुद्दत तक वो काग़ज़ नम रहा

सुबहे-पीरी[5] शाम होने आई मीर
तू न चेता यॉँ[6] बहुत दिन कम रहा

Gham raha jab tak ki dam mein dam raha
dil ke jaane ka nihayat gham raha

Zulfen khole tu to tuk aaya nazar
umra bhar yaan kaame-dil barhum raha

Uske lab se talkh hum sunte rahe
mere haq mein aabe-hevan sam raha

Mere rone ki haqiqat jismein thi
ek muddat tak woh kaghaz nam raha

Subhe-piri shaam hone aayi Meer
tu ne cheta yaan bahut din kam raha

---

1. आन्दोलित 2. कड़वा 3. अमृत 4. ज़हर 5. बुढ़ापा 6. यहाँ

As long as I was alive, sorrow and I could never part
All my life I grieved for the loss of my heart

Just for a while you showed up with your hair floating
And all my life, this heart was on you doting

From her lovely lips, only a hail of abuses came
From the heavenly fount, nothing but poison sprung
in nectar's name

The page on which it was written that I wept
For a long time a feel of moisture kept

You heeded not, O Meer, and the evening of life
turns into night
Even this long life was too short for you to come right.

अश्क़ आँखों में कब नहीं आता
ख़ून आता है जब नहीं आता

होश जाता नहीं रहा लेकिन
जब वो आता है तब नहीं आता

सब्र था एक मूनसे-हिज्रां[1]
सो वो मुद्दत से अब नहीं आता

दिल से रुख़सत हुई कोई ख़ुशी
गिरिया[2] बेसबब नहीं आता

जी में क्या-क्या है अपने ऐ हमदम
पर सुखन ताबलब[3] नहीं आता

दूर बैठा गुबारे-मीर उससे
इश्क़ बिन ये अदब नहीं आता

Ashq aankhon mein kab nahin aata
khoon aata hai jab nahin aata

Hosh jaata nahin raha lekin
jab woh aata hai tab nahin aata

Sabre tha ek moonse-hizran
so woh muddat se ab nahin aata

Dil se rukhsat hui koi khushi
giriya besabub nahin aata

Ji mein kya-kya hai apne ae humdum
per sukhan tabalub nahin aata

Door baitha ghubare-meer us se
ishq bin ye adab nahin aata

---

1. विरह का साथी 2. रोना 3. ज़ुबान पर

Tears are always welling up in my eyes
Or else, it is blood that on pupils lies

I have my bearings intact otherwise
I lose them when he arrives

In hours of separation, patience was my only friend
For ages now, its helping hand it does not lend

All joy from my heart flies
Without some reason, nobody cries

Ask me not what all I have in my heart, O friend
But I cannot express my feelings or the thoughts a tongue lend

Where she sat, Meer's dust came not near
One learns etiquettes only in love, my dear.

पैग़ामे-ग़म जिगर का गुलज़ार तक न पहुँचा
नाला[1] मेरा चमन की दीवार तक न पहुँचा

उस आइने की मानिंद ज़गार[2] जिसको खावे
काम अपना उसके ग़म में दीदार तक न पहुँचा

ये बख़्ते-सब्ज़ देखो, बागे-ज़माना में से
पज़मुर्दा[3] गुल भी अपनी दस्तार[4] तक न पहुँचा

लबरेज़-शिकवा थे हम लेकिन हज़ूर तेरे
कारे-शिकायत अपना गुफ़तार[5] तक न पहुँचा

यूसुफ़ से लेके तागुल, फिर गुल से लेके ताशम्मा
ये हुस्न किसको लेके बाज़ार तक न पहुँचा

Paighame-gham jigar ka gulzar tak ne pahuncha
naala mera chaman ki diwar tak ne pahuncha

Us aayine ki manind zagaar jisko khawe
kaam apna uske gham mein didaar tak ne pahuncha

Ye bakhte-sabz dekho, baage-zamana mein se
pazmurda gul bhi apni dastaar tak ne pahuncha

Labrez-shikva the hum hazur tere
kaare-shikayat apna guftaar tak ne pahuncha

Yusuf se leke tagul, phir gul se leke tashamma
ye husn kisko leke bazar tak ne pahuncha

---

1. रोना-धोना 2. ज़ंग 3. मुरझाया हुआ 4. पगड़ी 5. इज़हार

As my wailing could not scale the garden's wall
The missive from my stricken heart could reach not
the grove at all

Like the mirror which is rust-eaten on its glassy part
Because of the sorrow covering my heart, my efforts
to meet her came to nought

Look at my luck wonderful, from the world's garden
Not even a faded flower, could I tuck on my turban

Thousands of complaints flooded my mind
But in your presence not a syllable could utterance
find

Be it a candle, a rose or it may be the legendary
Yusuf's case
Beauty has dragged everyone to the marketplace.

अब जो हसरते जवानी है
उम्रे-रफ़ता[1] की ये निशानी है

गिरिया[2] हर वक्त का नहीं है हेच[3]
दिल में कोई ग़मे-निहानी[4] है

हम कफ़सज़ार कैदी हैं वरना
ताचमन[5] एक परफ़शानी है

खाक़ थी मौजज़न जहाँ में और
हमको धोका ये था कि पानी है

यां हुए मीर हम बराबर खाक़
वां वही नाज़ो सरगरानी[6] है

Ab jo hasrate jawani hai
umre-rufta ki ye nishani hai

Giriya har waqt ka nahin hai hech
dil main koi ghame-nihani hai

Hum kafaszaar qaidi hain varna
tachaman ek perfashani hai

Khaaq thi maujzan jahan mein aur
humko dhoka ye tha ki paani hai

Yaan hue Meer hum barabar khaaq
Waan vahi naazo sargarani hai

1. पुराने वक्त 2. रोना-धोना 3. बेवजह 4. छुपा हुआ 5. चमन तक 6. बददिमागी

Longing for youth at this stage
Is a remnant, only of the long past age

My heart is stricken by a sorrow deep
Surely, not for nothing do I weep

In the cage confined we love to stay
Otherwise the garden is only a flight away

It was only dust that floated around everywhere
We mistook it for shimmering water

She stays as usual arrogant and angry
While I am reduced to dust virtually.

क्या करूं शरह[1] खस्ताजानी[2] की
मैंने मर मर के ज़िन्दगानी की

हाले-बद[3] गुफ़्तनी[4] नहीं मेरा
तुमने पूछा तो मेहरबानी की

तिश्ना-लब[5] मर गये तेरे आशिक़
न मिली एक बूंद पानी की

जिससे खोई थी नींद 'मीर' ने कल
इब्तदा[6] फिर वही कहानी की

Kya karun shareh khastajani ki
maine mer mer ke zindgani ki

Haale-bad guftani nahin mera
tumne puchha to meharbani ki

Tishna-lab mar gaye tere aashiq
ne mili ek boond paani ki

Jisse khoi thi nind 'Meer' ne kal
ibtada phir wahi kahani ki

---

1. व्याख्या 2. अति दुख 3. बुरा हाल 4. कथनीय 5. प्यासे 6. आरंभ

How shall I my misery convey
All my life, I died everyday

My wretchedness is beyond description
Thanks indeed for enquiring about my condition

Thirsting for it, died your lover
Nobody gave him a drop of water

Because of which Meer lost sleep yesterday
The same story is beginning again today.

मुँह तका ही करे है जिस-तिस का
हैरती है ये आइना किसका

शाम ही से बुझा-सा रहता है
दिल हुआ है चराग़ मुफ़लिस का

थे बुरे मुग़बचों[1] के तेवर लेक[2]
शेख़ मैखाने से चला भागा

दाग़ आँखों के खिल रहे हैं सब
हाथ दस्ता हुआ है नरगिस का

ताब किसको कि हाले मीर सुने
हाल और कुछ है मजलिस का

Munh taka hi kare hai jis-tis ka
hairati hai ye aayina kiska

Sham hi se bujha-sa rehta hai
dil hua hai charag muflis ka

The bure mugbachon ke tewer lake
sheikh maikhane se chala bhaaga

Daagh aankhon ke khil rahe hain sub
haath dasta hua hai nargis ka

Taab kisko ki haale Meer sune
haal aur kuchh hai mazlis ka

1. मैखाने में काम करने वाले लड़के 2. गुस्से में

The mirror keeps looking at each and every person's face
Who is the wonderman it seeks to embrace

As the evening falls, it goes dim and dull
My heart is like a poor man's candle

The tavern-boys were in a furious mood
The Sheikh wisely out of the tavern moved

My wounds through my eyes unfold
A bouquet of narcissus in my hand I hold

Who will listen to Meer's tale here
The gathering seeks a different fare.

तेरे बन्दे हैं हम, खुदा जानता है
खुदा जाने तू हमको क्या जानता है

नहीं इश्क़ का दर्द लज़्ज़त से खाली
जिसे ज़ौक[1] हो वो मज़ा जानता है

मेरे दिल में रहता है तू ही तभी तो
जो कुछ दिल का है मुद्दआ जानता है

जफ़ा उनसे करता है हद से ज़्यादा
जिन्हें यार अहले-वफ़ा जानता है

जहाँ मीर आशिक़ हुआ ख्वार ही था
ये सौदाई कब दिल लगा जानता है

Tere bande hain hum, khuda jaanta hai
khuda jaane tu humko kya jaanta hai

Nahin ishq ka dard lazzat se khali
jise zauk ho woh maza jaanta hai

Mere dil mein rehta hai tu hi tabhi to
jo kuchh dil ka hai muddaa jaanta hai

Jafa unse karta hai hud se zayada
jinhen yaar ahle-wafa jaanta hai

Jahan Meer aashiq hua khwar hi tha
ye saudai kab dil laga jaanta hai

1. शौक

I am your humble servant, God knows it well
And what you think of me, only God can tell

Love's anguish too is with a rare joy knit
He alone who has loved can vouch for it

You reside in my heart, that is the reason
You know the wish that is therein hidden

He whose love for her is true and sincere
Gets from my beloved a treatment harsh and severe

Meer in love is always suffering
Just infatuated, he knows not the art of loving.

देख कि दिल की जां से उठता है
ये धुआं-सा कहाँ से उठता है

गोर[1] किस दिल जले की है ये फलक[2]
शोला इक सुबह यां से उठता है

बैठने कौन दे है फिर उसको
जो तेरे आस्तां[3] से उठता है

यूं उठे आह उस गली से हम
जैसे कोई जहाँ से उठता है

इश्क़ मीर एक भारी पत्थर है
कब ये तुझ नातवा[4] से उठता है

Dekh ki dil ki jaan se Uthta hai
ye dhuan-sa kahan se uthta hai

Gor kis dil jale ki hai ye phalak
shola ik subah yaan se uthta hai

Baithne kaun de hai phir usko
jo tere aastaan se uthta hai

Yun uthe aah us gali se hum
jaise koi jahan se uthta hai

Ishq Meer ek bhari pathar hai
kab ye tujh naatva se uthta hai

---

1. कब्र 2. आसमां 3. दर 4. कमज़ोर

Whether it rises from the soul or the heart
Just see from where doth this smoke-like thing start

Whose grave could it be O heaven
A flame rises from here every morning

He who once your threshold leaves
From nowhere any succour receives

So I left alas, from that street
As somebody from world would retreat

Love O Meer, is a load too heavy
To be carried by a frail man like thee.

कोफ़्त[1] से जान लब पे आई है
हमने क्या चोट दिल पे खाई है

लिखते रुक्का, लिखे गये दफ़्तर
शौक ने बात क्या बढ़ाई है

दीदनी[2] है शिकस्तगी[3] दिल की
क्या इमारत ग़मों ने ढाई है

जिस मरज़ से कि जान जाती है
दिलबरों की वो जुदाई है

मरगे-मजनू[4] पे अक्ल गुम है मीर
क्या दीवाने ने मौत पाई है

Kopht se jaan lab pe aayi hai
humne kya chot dil pe khayi hai

Likhte rukka, likhe gaye dafter
shauk ne baat kya badhai hai

Deedni hai shikastgi dil ki
kya imarat ghamon ne dhayi hai

Jis marz se ki jaan jaati hai
dilbaron ki woh judai hai

Marge-majnu pe akal gum hai Meer
kya diwane ne maut paayi hai

---

1. कष्ट 2. देखने के काबिल 3. दुर्दशा 4. मजनू की मौत

I have been by sorrows just undone
What a blow my heart has taken

I have given a whole discourse, though I wanted
only to write a letter
Love has so much expanded the matter

A sight in itself is my poor heart
What a mansion have sorrows to the ground brought

Separation from those close to our heart
Is a malady that can our demise cause

Mind-boggling O Meer is Majnu's demise
O what a death this lover dies.

आ जायें हम नज़र कोई दिन बहुत है यां
मौहलत बसाने-वर्को-शरर[1] कम बहुत है यां

यक लहज़ा[2] सीनाकोबी[3] से फुर्सत नहीं हमें
यानी कि दिल के जाने का मातम बहुत है यां

हासिल है क्या सिवाये तराई के दहर[4] में
उठ आसमां तले से कि शबनम बहुत है यां

इस बुतकदे में मानी का किससे करें सवाल
आदम नहीं है सूरत-आदम बहुत हैं यां

शायद कि काम सुबह तक अपना खिंचे न मीर
अहवाल[5] आज शाम से दरहम[6] बहुत है यां

Aa jaayen hum nazar koi din bahut hai yaan
mauhalt basane-varko-sharer kam bahut hai yaan

Yak lehza seenakobi se phursat nahin humein
yaani ki dil ke jaane ka maatam bahut hai yaan

Haasil hai kya siwaye taraai ke dehar mein
utha aasmaan tale se ki shabnam bahut hai yaan

Is butkade mein maani ka kisse karein sawal
aadam nahin hai surate-aadam bahut hain yaan

Shayad ki kaam subah tak apna khinche ne Meer
ahwaal aaj shaam se darhum bahut hai yaan

1. बुझती हुई चिंगारी या चमकती बिजली 2. एक क्षण 3. छाती पीटना 4. बुतखाना 5. हालत
6. बुरा, बिगड़ा हुआ

Like a flash of lightning or a dying spark we sojourn here
More than this we no more have time to stand and stare

No respite from beating our breast we receive
For the loss of our heart, we ceaselessly grieve

Man's lot in this world is but a moist eye
So much dew is falling here, get up from under the sky

Expect no understanding in the world from anywhere
For, mere human forms rather than human beings are seen here

I don't think O Meer, I'll last till the morning
Because I have been badly off right since this evening.

बरंगे[1]-बूए-गुल इस बाग़ के हम आशना[2] होते
कि हमराहे-सब टुक सैर करते फिर हवा होते

सरापा[3]-आरज़ू होने ने बंदा कर दिया हमको
वगरना[4] हम खुदा थे गर दिले-बेमुद्दआ[5] होते

फ़लक ऐ काश हम को खाक़ ही रखता कि इससे हम
गुबारे-राह होते या किसी की खाके-पा होते

इलाही[6] कैसे होते हैं जिन्हें है बंदगी की ख़्वाहिश
हमें तो शर्म दामनगीर[7] होती है खुदा होते

अब ऐसे हैं कि साने[8] के मिज़ाज ऊपर बहम पहुँचे
जो खातिरख्वाह[9] अपने हम हुए होते तो क्या होते

Barange-bue-gul is baagh ke hum aashna hote
ki humraahe-sab tuk sair karte phir hawa hote

Sarapa-aarzoo hone ne banda kar diya humko
bagarna hum khuda the gar dile-bemuddaa hote

Phalak ae kaash hum ko khaaq hi rakhta ki isse hum
gubare raah hote ya kisee ki khaake paa hote

Ilaahi kaise hote hain jinhen hai bandgi ki khwahish
humein to sharm daamangeer hoti hai khuda hote

Ab aise hain ki saane ke mizaj ooper behum pahunche
Jo khatirkhwah apne hum hue hote to kya hote

---

1. की तरह 2. परिचित 3. सिर से पांव तक 4. वरना 5. बिना इच्छा के 6. ईश्वर 7. शर्म आती 8. रचयिता 9. बनाने वाले

How I wish I had been familiar with the garden like
floral scent
And in company with the morning breeze my life
had spent

I am human because desires are my being's essential
part
I would have been god incarnate but for my longing
heart

Heavens should have let us as dust remain
So that an access to somebody's feet we could gain

I don't understand O Lord, why people wish to be
worshipped
I would have been so embarrassed if in God's place
I had been seated

Such we are when made according to the
Creator's will
I wonder what we would have been like if we had
used our own skill.

इश्क़ में जी को सबरो-ताब कहां
उससे आंखें लगें तो ख्वाब कहां

हस्ती अपनी है बीच में पर्दा
हम न होवें तो फिर हिजाब[1] कहां

गिरिया-ए-शब[2] से सुर्ख हैं आंखें
मुझ बलानोश को शराब कहां

इश्क़ है आशिक़ों के जलने को
ये जहन्नुम[3] में है अज़ाब[4] कहां

इश्क़ का घर है मीर से आबाद
ऐसे फिर खनुमा खराब[5] कहां

Ishq mein ji ko sabro-taab kahan
usse aankhen lagen to khwaab kahan

Hasti apni hai beech mein parda
hum ne howen to phir hijaab kahan

Giriya-e-shab se surkh hain aankhen
Mujh balanosh ko sharaab kahan

Ishq hai aashiqon ke jalne ko
ye jahannum mein hai azaab kahan

Ishq ka ghar hai Meer se aabaad
aise phir khanuma kharaab kahan

---

1. पर्दा 2. रात के रोने-धोने से 3. नर्क 4. कष्ट 5. उजड़े हुए घर वाले

Love takes one's peace and patience away
A lover can neither sleep by night nor rest by day

Our self is a veil between us and realization
But for this, there would be illumination

My eyes are red because at night I wept and did not sleep
How can a poor man like me afford to drink so deep!

The fires of hell can hardly match
The one that the lovers on earth catch

It is because of Meer that love exists in this world
Of how many house-wrecked men have you otherwise heard!

ऐ दोस्त कोई मुझ-सा रुसवा[1] न हुआ होगा
दुश्मन से भी दुश्मन पर ऐसा न हुआ होगा

टुक[2] गोरे-ग़रीबां[3] की कर सैर कि दुनिया में
इन ज़ुल्म-रसीदों[4] पर क्या-क्या न हुआ होगा

इस कुहना-ख़राबे[5] में आबादी न कर मुनहम
इक शहर नहीं था जो सहरा न हुआ होगा

जुज़[7] मरतबा-ए-कुल को हासिल कर ले है आखिर
इक क़तरा न देखा जो दरिया न हुआ होगा

सद नश्तरे-मिज़गां[8] के लगने से न निकला ख़ूं
आगे तुझे मीर ऐसा सौदा[9] न हुआ होगा

Ae dost koi mujh-sa ruswa ne hua hoga
dushman se bhi dushman per aisa ne hua hoga

Tuk gore ghariban ki kar sair ki duniya mein
in zulm-rasidon per kya-kya ne hua hoga

Is kuhna-kharabe mein aabaadi ne kar munhum
ik shaher nahin tha jo sehra ne hua hoga

Juz martaba-e-kul ko haasil kar le hai aakhir
ik qatra ne dekha jo dariya ne hua hoga

Sad nashtare-mizgaan ke lagne se ne nikla khoon
aage tujhe Meer aisa sauda ne hua hoga

1. बदनाम 2. ज़रा 3. ग़रीबों की कब्रें 4. दुख के मारे 5. बुरी दुनिया 6. अमीर, दयालु 7. हिस्सा 8. नयनों के तीर 9. पागलपन

Nobody O friend, would have met with such disgrace
Not even the worst of enemies would have passed through such a phase

Just a visit to the poor men's graves and you would have known
What atrocities of the world they must have borne

Do not build a home, you the rich, in this bad old world
There was not a town here which was not into wilderness hurled

Every part became a whole sooner or later
There is not a drop that did not become a river

You have had a thousand cuts from her eyes, but no blood came out
Before this, O Meer, you must not have gone through insanity's so severe a bout.

एक शे'र

शिकवा-ए-आबला[1] अभी से मीर
है प्यारे हनूज़ दिल्ली दूर

Shikva-ẹ-aablaa abhi se Meer
hai pyare hanooz dilli door

A Couplet

Of blisters in the feet, O Meer, you are complaining already
Quite some distance from here, my love, is as yet Delhi.

रुबाई

दामन उज़लत[1] का अब लिया मैंने
दिल मर्ग[2] से आशना[3] किया मैंने

था चश्मा-ए-आबे-ज़िंदगानी[4] नज़दीक
पर ख़ाक से उसको भर दिया मैंने

Daaman ujlat ka ab liya maine
dil marg se aashna kiya maine

Tha chashma-e-aabe-zindgani nazdeek
per khaak se usko bhar diya maine

1. एकांत 2. मृत्यु 3. परिचित 4. जीवन के लिए अमृत का चश्मा

A quartrain

I have embraced solitude now
And am in thoughts of my death lost

A fount of nectar beside me once lay
But I have filled it with dust and clay.

कारे-दिल मुझे उस महे-तमाम[1] से है
काहिरा[2] इक रोज़ मुझको शाम से है

तुम नहीं फ़ितना-नाज़[3] सच साहिब
शहर पुरशोर मुझ गुलाम से है

कोई तुझ-सा भी काश तुझको मिले
मुद्दआ हमको इंतकाम[4] से है

शे'र मेरे हैं सब ख्वास-पसंद[5]
गुफ़तगू पर मुझे अवाम से है

सहल है मीर को समझना क्या
हर सुखन[6] उसका इक मकाम से है

Kaare-dil mujhe us mahe-tamaam se hai
kahira ik roz mujhko shaam se hai

Tum nahin phitna-naaz such sahib
shaher purshor mujh gulaam se hai

Koi tujh-sa bhi kaash tujhko mile
muddaa humko intkaam se hai

She'r mere hain sab khwaas-pasand
guftgu per mujhe awaam se hai

Sehal hai Meer ko samajhna kya
her sukhan uska ik makaam se hai

1. पूरा चांद 2. तकलीफ़ 3. मुसीबत की जड़ 4. बदला 5. विशिष्ट लोगों के लिए 6. बात

Favour from that full waxing moon my heart wants
to gain
From evening itself it begins to pain

You are just not the cause of any mischief, sir
It is because of this slave that the town is in stir

Someone like yourself may you meet
For, all I want is vengeance sweet

Though my verses are meant for the select few
It is the common man that they are addressed to

Understanding Meer is not easy
Every verse of his tells a story.

यार बिन तल्ख[1] ज़िन्दगानी थी
दोस्ती मुद्दई-ए-जानी[2] थी

लुत्फ़ पर उसके हमनशीं[3] मत जा
कभू हम पर भी मेहरबानी थी

हाथ आता जो तू तो क्या होता
बरसों तक हमने ख़ाक छानी थी

मेरे क़िस्से से सब की गयीं नींदें
कुछ अजब तौर की कहानी थी

फुक्र[4] पर भी था 'मीर' के इक रंग
कफ़नी पहनी सो जाफ़रानी[5] थी

Yaar bin talkh zindgani thi
dosti muddai-e-jaani thi

Lutf per uske humnashin mat jaa
kabhu hum per bhi meharbani thi

Haath aata jo tu to kya hota
barson tak humne khaaq chhani thi

Mere kisse se sab ki gayee neenden
kuchh ajab taur ki kahani thi

Phukr per bhi tha 'Meer' ke ik rang
Kaphni pehni si jaaphrani thi

---

1. कड़वी 2. जान की दुश्मन 3. दोस्त 4. फ़कीरी 5. केसरिया

His friendship though was my life's cross
Without him too, this life was hard to pass

Let her favour O friend, not flatter you
At one time, she was kind to me too

What if ultimately I had been able to find
All my life, I had slogged for it and pined

So interesting was my tale, it had such a sway
That it took people's sleep away

Their apparel also was of saffron hue
Meer influenced the mendicants too.

आलम में कोई दिल का तलबगार न पाया
इस जिंस का यां हमने खरीदार न पाया

हक़[1] ढूंढने का आपको आता नहीं वरना
आलम है सभी यार कहां यार न पाया

सूराख़ है सीने में हर इक शख़्स के तुझ से
किस दिल के तेरा तीरे-निगह पार न पाया

आईना भी हैरत से मुहब्बत में हुए हम
पर सेर[2] हो उस शख़्स का दीदार न पाया

वह खैंच के शमशीरे-सितम रह गया जो 'मीर'
खूंरेज़ी[3] का यां कोई सज़ावार[4] न पाया

Aalam mein koi dil ka talabgaar ne paya
is jins ka yaan humne kharidaar ne paya

Haq dhundhne ka aapko aata nahin varna
aalam hai sabhi yaar kahan yaar ne paya

Suraakh hai sine mein her ik shakhs ke tujh se
kis dil ke tera teere-nigah paar ne paya

Aayina bhi hairat se muhabbat ki hue hum
per ser ho us shakhs ka deedaar ne paya

Woh khainch ke shamsheere-sitam reh gaya jo 'Meer'
khunrezee ka yaan koi sazawaar ne paya

---

1. अधिकार 2. जी भर कर 3. खून 4. पात्र

I find nobody in the world who my heart's feeling
reads
This is a commodity that no customer needs

You have no urge to quest otherwise you would
certainly come by
Friends and friends wherever you try

Everybody has a hole in the heart because of you
I find nobody who has not been by the arrow from
your eye pierced through

I became even a mirror in love, so far I went
Still her face I did not see to my heart's content

O Meer, even when she flashed a naked sword of
cruelty
She wasn't even then for bloodshed held guilty.

इधर से अब्र[1] उठकर जो गया है
हमारी ख़ाक पर भी रो गया है

मुसायब[2] और थे, पर दिल का जाना
अजब इक सानहा[3] सा हो गया है

सिरहाने 'मीर' के कोई न बोलो
अभी टुक रोते-रोते सो गया है।

Idhar se abra uthkar jo gaya hai
humari khaaq per bhi ro gaya hai

Musayab aur the, per dil ka jaana
ajab ik saanha sa ho gaya hai

Sirhane 'Meer' ke koi ne bolo
abhi tuk rote-rote so gaya hai

---

1. बादल 2. मुसीबतें 3. दुर्घटना

The cloud that just passed from here
Has on my dust also shed a tear

I had troubles enough already
But falling in love is indeed a tragedy

May nobody at Meer's bedside speak
He was weeping and has just fallen asleep

इस बाग़े-बेसबात[1] में क्या दिल सबा[2] लगे
क्या-क्या निहाल[3] देखते यां पांव आ लगे

किसको खबर है कश्ती-तबाहों के हाल की
तख़्ता मगर[4] किनारे कोई बह के जा लगे

मक़सूद[5] के ख़याल में बहुतों ने छानी ख़ाक
आलम तमाम वहम है यां हाथ क्या लगे

सब चाहते हैं देर रहे 'मीरे-दिलज़दा'[6]
या रब किसी तो दोस्त की उसको दुआ लगे

Is baaghe-basebaat mein kya dil saba lage
kya-kya nihaal dekhte yaan paon aa lage

Kisko khaber hai kashti-tabahon ke haal ki
takhta magar kinare koi beh ke jaa lage

Maqsood ke khyaal mein bahuton ne chani khaaq
aalam tammam vehum hai yaan haath kya lage

Sub chahate hain der rahe 'Meere-dilzada'
yaarub kisoo to dost ki usko dua lage

---

1. नश्वर बाग (संसार) 2. सुबह की हवा 3. पौधे 4. शायद 5. लक्ष्य (प्रियतम, ईश्वर) 6. दुखी 'मीर'

Razed to the ground when you see such lofty trees
How can you feel at home in such a perishable
garden, O morning breeze

Who can feel the plight of the boat-wrecked sore,
Whose only hope is that some plank floats along and
reaches the shore

Thousands have given their life in order that their
goal they attain
But what can you expect from a world which is only
an illusion and what can you possibly retain

Meer, the miserable has lived too long, the people
say
May God some sincere friend's prayer now take him
away.

सोजिशे-दिल से मुफ़्त जलते हैं
दाग़ जैसे चराग़ जलते हैं

भरी आती हैं आज यूं आंखें
जैसे दरिया कहीं उबलते हैं

दमे-आखिर[1] है बैठ जा, मत जा
सब्र कर टुक कि हम भी चलते हैं

तेरे बेखुद[2] जो हैं सो क्या चेतें
ऐसे डूबे कहीं उछलते हैं!

'मीर' साहब को देखिए जो बने
अब बहुत घर से कम निकलते हैं

Sojishe-dil se mupht jalte hain
daagh jaise charaag jalte hain

Bhari aati hain aaj yoon aankhen
jaise dariya kahin ubalte hain

Dame-aakhir hai baith jaa, mat jaa
sabra kar tuk ki hum bhi chalte hain

Tere bekhud jo hain so kya cheten
aise doobe kahin uchhalte hain!

'Meer' saheb ko dekhiye jo bane
ab bahut ghar se kam nikatle hain

---

1. अंत समय 2. आत्म-विस्मृत

Due to the heat in my heart, soft they turn
Like candles do my spots burn

Today, like rivers in spate
My eyes with tears fill, and inflate

I am breathing my last, please do not from me part
Stay a little longer, for I'm about to depart

I lose my bearings, I am so lost in your thought
People so drowned, come out not

If possible, do look up Meer Sahib
Rarely out of his house now, stirs he.

आरज़ूएं हज़ार रखते हैं
तो भी हम दिल को मार रखते हैं।

बर्क़[1] कम-हौसला है, हम भी तो
दिले-बेक़रार[2] रखते हैं

न निगह, न पयाम, न वादा
नाम को हम भी यार रखते हैं

हमसे ख़ुश-ज़मां[3] कहां, यूं तो
लबो-लहजा[4] हज़ार[5] रखते हैं

फिर भी करते हैं 'मीर' साहब इश्क़
हैं जवां, इख़्तियार रखते हैं।

Aarzooen hazaar rakhte hain
to bhi hum dil ko maar rakhte hain

Bark kam-hausla hai, hum bhi to
dile-beqaraar rakhte hain

Na nigah, na payaam, na vaada
naam ko hum bhi yaar rakhte hain

Hum se khush-zamaan kahan, yoon to
labo-lahaja hazaar rakhte hain

Phir bhi karte hain 'Meer' saheb ishq
hain jawan, ikhtiyaar rakhte hain

---

1. बिजली 2. बेचैन दिल 3. अच्छा गाने वाले 4. अच्छी आवाज़ 5. हज़ारों लोग या बुलबुल (हज़ार दास्तां)

I have desires countless
Which I somehow suppress

The lightning lacks courage or else let it strike
My heart, which is storm-like

Neither his sight, nor promise, nor a message from
him came
I too have a friend but only in name

Although many a one knows how himself to express
Who can match me in poetic prowess

Meer Sahib has not given up loving still
He keeps young and has his will.

करते हैं जो कि जी में ठाने हैं
खूबरू[1] किसकी बात माने हैं

जा हमें उस गली में गिर रहना
जोफ़ो-बेताक़ती[2] बहाने हैं

पूछ अहले-तरब[3] से शौक़ अपना
वे ही जानें जो खाक छाने हैं

इश्क़ करते हैं उस परीरू[4] से
'मीर' साहब भी क्या दिवाने हैं

Karte hain jo ki jee mein thane hain
khoobru kiski baat mane hain

Jaa humein us gali mein gir rehna
jopho-betaaqti bahane hein

Poochh ahle-tarab se shauq apna
ve hi jaanen jo khaaq chhane hain

Ishq karte hain us pariru se
'Meer' saheb bhi kya diwane hain

---

1. सुंदर लोग 2. कमज़ोरी 3. सुखी लोग 4. सुंदर प्रियतम

They do what they wish to be done
The handsome people listen to none

In any case, I would have been lying in her alley
My frailty was an excuse only

He alone knows who suffers and tries to find
No point asking the happy ones how it grinds

He has fallen for a fairy
Meer has gone mad, really.

है तहे-दिल[1] बुतों के क्या मालूम
निकले परदे से क्या खुदा मालूम

यही जाना कि कुछ न जाना हाय
सो भी इक उम्र में हुआ मालूम

इल्म सब को है यह कि सब तू है
फिर है अल्लाह कैसा ना मालूम

इश्क़ जाना था मार रक्खेगा
इब्तदा[2] में थी इंतहा[3] मालूम

इश्क़ है ऐ तबीब[4] जी का रोग
लुत्फ़[5] कर है जो कुछ दवा मालूम

Hai tahe-dil buton ke kya maloom
nikle parde se kya khuda maloom

Yahi jaana ki kuchh na jaana haaye
so bhi ik umra mein hua maloom

Ilm sab ko hai yeh ki sab tu hai
phir hai allah kaisa naa maloom

Ishq jaana tha maar rakhega
ibtada mein thi inteha maloom

Ishq hai ae tabeeb ji ka rog
lutf kar hai jo kuchh dava maloom

1. दिल के अन्दर 2. आरंभ 3. अंत 4. चिकित्सक 5. कृपा

What lies hidden in the human heart, nobody has seen
Who knows what emerges from behind the screen

All that I know is that I know nothing
And it took me a long age to know this simple thing

It is all because of God, all that we see
But nobody knows how looks He

In the beginning itself the end-result I knew
I knew that love would take my life too

Love is a disease of the heart, O physician
Please tell me if you know any medicine.

सब सरगुज़श्त[1] सुन चुके अब चुपके हो रहो
आख़िर[2] हुई कहानी मेरी तुम भी सो रहो

जोशे-मुहीते-इश्क़ में क्या जी से गुफ़्तगू
इस गौहरे-गिरामी[3] से अब हाथ धो रहो

इतना सियाह-ख़ानए-आशिक़[4] से नंग[5] क्या
कितने दिनों में आये हो यां रात तो रहो

खतरा बहुत है 'मीर' रहे-सअबे-इश्क़[6] में
ऐसा न हो कहीं कि दिलो-दीं को खो रहो

Sub sarguzasht sun chuke ab chupke ho raho
aakhir hui kahani meri tum bhi so raho

Joshe-muhite-ishq mein kya ji se guftgu
is gauhare-girami se ab haath dho raho

Itna siyaah-khane-aashiq se nang kya
kitne dino mein aaye ho yaan raat to raho

Khatra bahut hai 'Meer' rahe-sa-abe-ishq mein
aisa ne ho kahin ki dilo-deen ko kho raho

---

1. कहानी 2. समाप्त 3. कीमती मोती 4. प्रेमी के अन्धेरे घर 5. शर्म 6. प्रेम का कठिन मार्ग

You have heard my tale, so better, be silent, pray
And sleep now because I have said whatever I had to say

When the tide of love rises, what dialogue can you have with the heart
In that state, take this precious pearl as good as lost

Why feel shy in this house of love, sans all light
You have come after so many days, stay at least for a night

The path of love is indeed with dangers fraught
Take care O Meer, lest you should lose both your faith and the heart.

बंधा रात आंसू का कुछ तार सा
हुआ अब्रे-रहमत[1] गुनहगार सा

कोई सादा[2] ही उसको सादा कहे
लगे है हमें तो वो अय्यार[3] सा

मुहब्बत है या कोई जी का है रोग
सदा मैं तो रहता हूं बीमार सा

मगर[4] आंख तेरी भी चिपकी कहीं
टपकता है चितवन से कुछ प्यार सा

नहीं 'मीरे'-मस्ताना सोहबत का बाब[5]
मुसाहिब करो कोई हुशियार सा

Bandha raat aansu ka kuchh taar sa
hua abre-rehmat gunehgaar sa

Koi saada hi usko saada kahe
lage hai humen to woh ayyaar sa

Muhabbat hai ya koi ji ka hai rog
sada main to rehta hoon bimaar sa

Magar aankh teri bhi chipki kahin
tapakta hai chitvan se kuchh pyaar sa

Nahin 'Meere'-mastana sohbat ka baab
musahib karo koi hushiyaar sa

---

1. दैवी कृपा का बादल 2. मूर्ख, भोला 3. चालाक 4. शायद 5. लायक

Tears from my eyes last night flowed so steadily
That they overwhelmed even the cloud of God's mercy

Only for a simpleton is he a simple person
I found him rather a clever and cunning one

Is it love or heart's malady
I remain always sickly

Perhaps you are in love with somebody
Your face shows it clearly

Meandering Meer will not do for a companion
For that you choose a smart person.

जब भी पहलू से यार उठता है
दर्द बेइख़तयार उठता है

अब तलक भी मज़ारे-मजनू से
नातवां इक गुबार उठता है
है बगूला गुबार किसका मीर
कि जो हो बेकरार उठता है

Jab bhi pehlu se yaar uthta hai
dard beikhtyaar uthta hai

Ab talak bhi mazaare-majnu se
naatvan ik gubaar uthta hai

Hai bagula gubaar kiska Meer
ki jo ho bekarar uthta hai

When my love leaves my side
I am grief stricken, woe-betied

From Majnu's grave, they say
A thin cloud of dust rises till this day

Most restlessly it goes
From where O Meer, this cloud of dust blows.

या रब! कोई हो इश्क़ का बीमार न होवे
मर जाय वले[1] उसको ये आज़ार न होवे

ज़िंदां[2] में फंसे, तौक़ पड़े, क़ैद में मर जाए
पर दामे-मुहब्बत[3] में गिरफ़्तार न होवे

इस वास्ते कांपूँ हूं कि हैं आह निपट सर्द
यह बाउ[4] कलेजे के कहीं पार न होवे

सहराए-मुहब्बत[5] है, क़दम देख के रख 'मीर'
यह सैर सरे-कूचा-ओ-बाज़ार[6] न होवे

Yaa rub! koi ho ishq ka bimaar na howe
mar jaaye wale usko ye aazaar na howe

Zindan mein phanse, tauq pare, qaid mein mar jaaye
per daame-muhabbat mein giraftaar na howe

Is waaste kaampoon hoon ki hain aah nipat sard
yeh baau kaleje ke kahin paar na howe

Sehrae-muhabbat hai, kadam dekh ke rakh 'Meer'
yeh sair sare-kucha-o-bazaar na howe

---

1. किन्तु 2. कैद 3. प्रेमजाल 4. वायु 5. प्रेम का जंगल 6. गलियों और बाजारों की सैर

May God, nobody should be by love stricken
He should rather be dead than by this malady undone

He should rather be in fetters, be in prison and die there
But never be caught in love's snare

My sigh is cold like ice and I shiver
It might rent my heart, I fear

It is the desert of love, O Meer, so carefully tread
It is not a walk through the market or common street that lies ahead.

ज़ुबां रख गुल-सा[1] अपने दहन[2] में
बंधी मुट्ठी चली जा इस चमन से

न तुझ बिन होश में हम आये साक़ी
मुसाफिर ही रहे अकसर वतन में

खिरदमंदी[3] हुई ज़ंजीर, वरना
गुज़रनी खूब थी दीवानापन में

कहाँ अजिज़[4] सुख कादिर-सुखन[5] हूँ
हमें है शुबहा यारों के सुखन में

गुदाज़े-इश्क़[6] में बह भी गया मीर
यही धोखा-सा है अब पैरहन[7] में

Zuban rakh gul-sa apne dehan mein
bandhi mutthi chali jaa is chaman se

Na tujh bin hosh mein hum aaye saaqi
musafir hi rahe aksar vatan mein

Khirdmandi hui zanjeer, varna
gujzarni khoob thi diwanapan mein

Kahan ajiz sukh kadir-sukhan hoon
humein hai shubha yaaro ke sukhan mein

Gudaze-ishq mein beh bhi gaya Meer
yahi dhokha-sa hai ab pairhan mein

---

1. फूल जैसा 2. मुँह 3. अक्लमंदी 4. बेचारा 5. शायरी में उस्ताद 6. इश्क़ की गर्मी 7. पोशाक

Keep your tongue in your mouth shut, and so
With your palms closed into the garden go

Without you, O saqi we felt bewildered and lost
Stranger-like we remained in our own home for the most part

We were restrained by the demands of sanity
Otherwise we would have had a gala time in a state of frenzy

Far from being a novice, I am a master of poetry
I suspect my critics could not my merit see

In the fires of love, Meer has melted away already
Inside his clothes now there is an illusion only.

ग़ैरों से मिल चले तुम मस्ते-शराब होकर
ग़ैरत से रह गए हम यकसू[1] कबाब होकर

कल रात मुंद गयी थी बहुतों की आँख गश से
देखा किया न कर तू सर-मस्ते-ख्वाब[2] होकर

इक क़तरा आब मैंने इस दौर में पिया है
निकला है चश्मे-तर से वो खूने-नाब[3] होकर

आ बैठता था सूफ़ी हर सुबह मैकदे में
शुक्रे-खुदा कि निकला वां से खराब होकर

शर्मे-हया कहाँ तक, हैं मीर कोई दम के
अब तो मिला करो तुम टुक बेनकाब होकर

Ghairon se mil chale tum maste-sharaab hokar
ghairat se reh gaye hum yaksu kabbab hokar

Kal raat mund gayi thi bahuton ki aankh gash se
dekha kiya ne kar tu sar-maste-khwab hokar

Ik qatra aab maine is daur mein piya hai
nikla hai chashme-tar se woh khoone-naab hokar

Aa baithta tha sufi her subah maiqade mein
shukre-khuda ki nikla vaan se kharaab hokar

Sharme-haya kahan tak, hain Meer Koi dam ke
ab to mila karo tum tuk benakaab hokar

---

1. एकदम 2. नींद का माल 3. शुद्ध रक्त

You met others as if drunk with wine
And like roasted meat burnt with jealousy this heart of mine

Many a one fell unconscious last night and some did actually die
Look not at people pray with a dreamy eye

If even a drop of water in this time in my stomach goes
Like pure blood from my eyes it flows

Thank God he has gone humbled out of the tavern
He would come and sit there right in the morning, that abstemious one

Why feel shy before him, Meer's life now is but a few day's tale
Now at least you should meet him without the veil.

कद्र रखती न थी मता-ए-दिल[1]
सारे आलम में मैं दिखा लाया

दिल कि इक क़तरा खूं नहीं है बेश[2]
एक आलम के सर बला लाया

इब्तदा में ही मर गये सब यार
इश्क़ की कौन इन्तहा लाया

सब पे जिस बार ने गरानी[3] की
उसको मैं नातवां[4] उठा लाया

अब तो जाते हैं मैक़दे से मीर
फिर मिलेंगे अगर खुदा लाया

Kadra rakhti na thi mata-e-dil
saare aalam mein main dikha laaya

Dil ki ik qatra khoon nahin hai besh
ek aalam ke sar bala laaya

Ibtada mein hi mar gaye sub yaar
ishq ki kaun inteha laaya

Sub pe jis baar ne garani ki
usko main naatvan utha laaya

Ab to jaate hain maiqade se Meer
Phir milenge agar khuda laaya

1. दिल की दौलत 2. बाकी 3. भारीपन 4. कमज़ोर

The heart seems to command little worth
I have displayed it all over the earth

Not a drop of blood in the heart doth remain
I was cursing the whole world in vain

My comrades deserted this path in the very start
To face the consequences of love, nobody had the heart

This frail man could carry
The load which was for everybody else too heavy

For now, O Meer, I bid good-bye to the tavern
It is for God to decide if and when I return.

मिलिए उस शख्स से जो आदम होवे
नाज़ उसको कमाल पर बहुत कम होवे

हो गर्मे-सुख़न तो गिर्द आवे एक खलक
खामोश रहे तो एक आलम होवे

Miliye us shakhs se jo aadam howe
naaz usko kamaal per bahut kam howe

Ho garme-sukhan to gird aawe ek khalak
khamosh rahe to ek aalam howe

Seek the man who is truly human
And is not proud of being a gifted one

The world should flock around him when he
speaks
And becomes a universe unto himself when
silence keeps.

मेरे संगे-मज़ार[1] पर फरहाद
रखके तेशा कहे है, या उस्ताद

फ़िक्रे तामीर में न रह मुनइम[2]
ज़िंदगानी की कुछ भी है बुनियाद?

सुनते हो, टुक सुनो कि फिर मुझ बाद
न सुनोगे ये नाला-ओ-फरियाद[3]

हर तरफ है असीर[4] हमआवाज़
बाग़ हैं घर तेरा तो ऐ सैयाद

हमको मरना ये है कि कब होवें
अपनी क़ैदे-हयात[5] से आज़ाद

Mere sange-mazaar per farhaad
rakhke tesha kahe hai, ya ustaad

Phikre taameer mein na rah munaim
zindgani ki kuchh bhi hai buniyaad

Sunte ho, tuk suno ki phir mujh baad
na sunoge ye naala-e-fariyaad

Her taraf hai aseer humawaaz
baagh hain ghar tera to ae saiyad

Humko marna ye hai ki kab howen
apni qaide-hayat se aazaad

---

1. कब्र का पत्थर 2. अमीर आदमी 3. रोना-धोना 4. कैदी 5. ज़िंदगी

As Farhad on my grave put his pick-axe
About my being a master, he could not but eloquently wax

Do not much store by your buildings and riches lay
Life is built on crumbling clay

Do hear me now, for, after I am no more found
You will never hear such plaints and wailing around

This garden is no garden, it is only your abode, O hunter
For, my fellow-birds are in cage everywhere

I am dying by this thought beset
When my release from life will I get.

था मुस्तआर[1] हुस्न से उसके जो नूर था
खुर्शीद[2] में भी उसका ही ज़र्रा[3] ज़हूर[4] था

पहुंचा जो आप[5] को तो मैं पहुंचा खुदा के तईं
मालूम यह हुआ कि बहुत मैं भी दूर था

कल पाँव एक कासा-ए-सर[6] पर जो आ गया
यकसर वो उस्तख़्वानों[7] शिकस्तों[8] से चूर था
कहने लगा कि देख के चल राह, बेखबर!
मैं भी कभू किसू का सरे-पुर-ग़रूर था

था वह तो रश्के-हूरे-बहिश्ती[9] हमीं में 'मीर'
समझे न हम तो फ़हम[10] का अपनी क़सूर था

Tha mustaar husn se uske jo noor tha
khurshid mein bhi uska hi zarra zahoor tha

Pahuncha jo aap ko to main pahuncha khuda ke taeen
Maloom yeh hua ki bahut main bhi door tha

Kal paon ek kaasa-e-sar per jo aa gaya
yaksar woh ustkhwanon shikaston se choor tha

Kehne laga ki dekh ke chal raah, bekhaber!
main bhi kabhu kisso ka sare-pur-gharoor tha

Tha veh to rashke-hure-bahisti humeen mein 'Meer'
samjhe ne hum to phahum ka apni kasoor tha

---

1. उधार लिया हुआ 2. सूर्य 3. किंचित् 4. प्रकट होना 5. स्वयं 6. खोपड़ी 7. हड्डी 8. चोटों 9. हूर को लजाने वाला प्रियतम (ईश्वर) 10. समझ

Whatever light the sun doth radiate
Is all because of God, the effulgent and great

When I understood myself I felt as if God Himself
I had seen
And then I realized how far even from myself I had
been

Yesterday when my foot came over a skull by chance
It was wounded by the sharp bone, and it said

Tread carefully thou the reckless one
I too was once a proud and puffed up head

The radiant one who was within me and would even
the hoors of heaven outshine
If I understood him not, the fault was entirely mine.

जिन-जिन को था ये इश्क़ का आज़ार मर गए
अक्सर हमारे साथ के बीमार मर गए

यूँ कानों-कान गुल[1] ने न जाना चमन में आह
सर को पटक के हम पसे-दीवार[2] मर गए

सद कारवाँ[3] वफ़ा है कोई पूछता नहीं
गोयां मता-ए-दिल[4] के ख़रीदार मर गए

मजनूं न दश्त[5] में हैं न फ़रहाद कोह[6] में
था जिन से लुत्फ़े ज़िन्दगी वे यार मर गए

घबरा न 'मीर' इश्क़ में इस सलह जीस्त[7] पर
जब बस चला न कुछ तो मेरे यार मर गए

Jin-jin ko tha ye ishq ka aazaar mar gaye
aksar humare saath ke bimaar mar gaye

Yoon kaanon-kaan gul ne na jaana chaman mein aah
sar ko patak ke hum pase-diwaar mar gaye

Sad karwaan wafa hai koi puchhta nahin
goyan mata-e-dil ke kharidaar mar gaye

Majnoon na dasht mein hai na farhaad koh mein
tha jin se lutfe zindgi ve yaar mar yage

Ghabra na 'Meer' ishq mein is salah jist per
jab bus chala na kuchh to mere yaar mar gaye

---

1. फूल (प्रियतम) 2. दीवार के पीछे 3. सैंकड़ों कारखानों में 4. दिल की दौलत 5. जंगल 6. पहाड़ 7. ज़िंदगी

All those stricken with love are dead
Dead all those, who lay beside our bed

Only the blossoms in the garden did not my sighs heed
I died, against the wall breaking my head

Sincerity, even hundredfold, no taker finds,
All those who valued the riches of the heart are dead

Neither is Majnu in the wild, nor Farhad on the hill we find
All of those, with whom this life was a joy, have gone ahead

Lose not your heart, O Meer, for those hardships of love
Our friends too, when helpless, chose to be dead.

फ़क़ीराना[1] आए सदा[2] कर चले
मियाँ खुश रहो हम दुआ कर चले

शफ़ा अपनी तक़दीर ही में न थी
कि मक़दूर[3] भर तो दवा कर चले

वो क्या चीज़ है आह जिसके लिए
हर इक चीज़ से दिल उठाकर चले

कोई ना-उमीदाना[4] करते निगाह
सो तुम हमसे मुँह भी छुपाकर चले

दिखाई दिये यूँ कि बेखुद[5] किया
हमें आपसे भी जुदा कर चले

कहें क्या जो पूछे कोई हमसे 'मीर'
जहाँ में तुम आए थे क्या कर चले

Fakirana aaye sada kar chale
miyan khush raho hum dua kar chale

Shapha apni taqdeer hi mein na thi
ki maqdoor bhar to dava kar chale

Woh kya cheez hai aah jiske liye
her ik cheez se dil uthakar chale

Koi na-umidaana karte nigaah
so tum humse munh bhi chhupakar chale

Dikhayi diye yoon ki bekhud kiya
humein aapse bhi juda kar chale

Kahen kya jo puchhe koi humse 'Meer'
Jahan mein tum aaye the kya kar chale

---

1. फ़क़ीरों की तरह 2. आवाज़ लगाना 3. ताक़त 4. निराशाहपूर्वक 5. आत्मविस्मृत

Like faqirs we came and gave our call
May you remain happy, one and all

The cure was just not for us decreed
We tried as much as we could, indeed

What is it after all, that could make
The man leave this world for its sake

You should have at least cast a glance, you may not have obliged
But even your face from me you chose to hide

Your very sight took our bearings away
You sundered us even from ourselves, so to say

What shall we say, Meer, if asked by someone
"You came to the world here, so what have you done?"

क्या काम किया हमने यूँ दिल न लगाना था
इस जान की जोखों को उस वक्त न जाना था

क्योंकर गली से उसकी मैं उठके चला जाता
या खाक में मिलना था लोहू में नहाना था

कहता था किसू से कुछ तकता था किसू का मुंह
कल 'मीर' खड़ा था याँ सच है कि दिवाना था

Kya kaam kiya humne yun dil na lagana tha
is jaan ki jokhon ko us waqt na jaana tha

Kyonkar gali se uski main uthke chala jaata
ya khaaq mein milna tha lohu mein nahana tha

Kehta tha kisoo se kuchh takta tha kisoo ka munh
kal 'Meer' khara tha yan sach hai ki diwana tha

लज़्ज़त से नहीं खाली जानों का खपा जाना
कब खिज़्रो-मसीहा[1] ने जीने का मज़ा जाना

कब बंदगी[2] मेरी सी बंदा करेगा कोई
जाने है खुदा उसको मैं तुझको खुदा जाना

था नाज़ बहुत हमको दानिस्त[3] पर अपनी भी
आखिर वो बुरा निकला हम जिसको भला जाना

ऐ शोरे-क़यामत[4] हम सोते ही न रह जाएं
इस राह से निकलो तो हमको भी जगा जाना

जाती है गुज़र जी पर उस वक़्त क़यामत सी
याद आवे है जब तेरा यक-बारगी आ जाना

Lazzat se nahin khali jaanon ka khapa jaana
kab khizro-masiha ne jeene ka maza jaana

Kab bandgi meri si banda karega koi
jaane hai khuda usko main tujhko khuda jaana

Tha naaz bahut humko daanist per apni bhi
aakhir woh bura nikla hum jisko bhala jaana

Ae shore-qayamat hum sote hi na reh jaayen
is raah se niklo to humko bhi jaga jaana

Jaati he guzar ji per us waqt qayamat si
yaad aawe hai jab tera yak-baargi aa jaana

---

1. हज़रत खिज्र और ईसा मसीह अमर माने गये हैं 2. उपासना 3. समझ 4. प्रलय-नाद

By falling in love what a silly thing I have done
I shouldn't have this nuisance for my life spun

I shouldn't have left her street and come here
Either I should have been reduced to dust or bathed in blood there

He would speak to somebody and look at somebody else's face
Truly mad, only yesterday Meer stood at this very place.

By falling in love what a silly thing I have done
I shouldn't have this nuisance for my life spun

I shouldn't have left her street and come here
Either I should have been reduced to dust or bathed in blood there

He would speak to somebody and look at somebody else's face
Truly mad, only yesterday Meer stood at this very place.

लज़्ज़त से नहीं खाली जानों का खपा जाना
कब खिज्रो-मसीहा[1] ने जीने का मज़ा जाना

कब बंदगी[2] मेरी सी बंदा करेगा कोई
जाने है खुदा उसको मैं तुझको खुदा जाना

था नाज़ बहुत हमको दानिस्त[3] पर अपनी भी
आखिर वो बुरा निकला हम जिसको भला जाना

ऐ शोरे-क़यामत[4] हम सोते ही न रह जाएं
इस राह से निकलो तो हमको भी जगा जाना

जाती है गुज़र जी पर उस वक़्त क़यामत सी
याद आवे है जब तेरा यक-बारगी आ जाना

Lazzat se nahin khali jaanon ka khapa jaana
kab khizro-masiha ne jeene ka maza jaana

Kab bandgi meri si banda karega koi
jaane hai khuda usko main tujhko khuda jaana

Tha naaz bahut humko daanist per apni bhi
aakhir woh bura nikla hum jisko bhala jaana

Ae shore-qayamat hum sote hi na reh jaayen
is raah se niklo to humko bhi jaga jaana

Jaati he guzar ji per us waqt qayamat si
yaad aawe hai jab tera yak-baargi aa jaana

---

1. हज़रत खिज्र और ईसा मसीह अमर माने गये हैं 2. उपासना 3. समझ 4. प्रलय-नाद

क्या काम किया हमने यूँ दिल न लगाना था
इस जान की जोखों को उस वक्त न जाना था

क्योंकर गली से उसकी मैं उठके चला जाता
या खाक में मिलना था लोहू में नहाना था

कहता था किसू से कुछ तकता था किसू का मुंह
कल 'मीर' खड़ा था याँ सच है कि दिवाना था

Kya kaam kiya humne yun dil na lagana tha
is jaan ki jokhon ko us waqt na jaana tha

Kyonkar gali se uski main uthke chala jaata
ya khaaq mein milna tha lohu mein nahana tha

Kehta tha kisoo se kuchh takta tha kisoo ka munh
kal 'Meer' khara tha yan sach hai ki diwana tha

Like faqirs we came and gave our call
May you remain happy, one and all

The cure was just not for us decreed
We tried as much as we could, indeed

What is it after all, that could make
The man leave this world for its sake

You should have at least cast a glance, you may not have obliged
But even your face from me you chose to hide

Your very sight took our bearings away
You sundered us even from ourselves, so to say

What shall we say, Meer, if asked by someone
"You came to the world here, so what have you done?"

Losing one's life in love is not without pleasure
Christ knew not the joys of life nor did Khizra

Which other human being can pray as I do
The world think that God is someone else,
I think it is you

What a great pride in my wisdom I had
But he who I thought was good, ultimately turned
out to be bad

Lest I should remain sleeping, O the din of doom's
. day
Do wake me up when you pass this way

Whenever I remember your arrival all of a sudden
It feels as if for me the day of judgment has come.

जो लोग आसमां ने याँ खाक कर उड़ाये
बे-इब्रतों[1] ने लेकर खाक उनकी घर बनाये

रहने की कोई जगह शायद न थी उन्हों के
जो याँ से उठ गये हैं फिर वे कभू न आये

लड़के बरहमनों के संदलभरी जबीनें[2]
हिन्दोस्तां में देखे सो उनसे दिल लगाये

आहे-शरर-फ़शां[3] जो निकले है मुंह से हरदम
रौशन[4] है 'मीर' ग़म ने क़ल्बो-कबद[5] जलाये

Jo log aasmaan ne yann khaak kar uraaye
be-ibraton ne lekar khaak unki ghar banaye

Rehne ki koi jagah shayad na thi unhon ki
jo yaan se uth gaye hain phir we kabhu ne aaye

Larke berehamnon ke sandalbhari jabine
hindostan mein dekhe so unse dil lagaye

Aahe-sharer-phashan jo nikle hai munh se hardum
roshan hai 'Meer' ghum ne qalbo-kabat jalaye

---

1. शिक्षा न लेने वालों 2. माथे 3. चिंगारी बरसाने वाली आह 4. स्पष्ट 5. दिल और कलेजा

Those whom heaven laid low under the earth
The unteachable ones reduced their houses also to dust

Perhaps there was no place for them to live anywhere
Those who left this world never came back here

The sons of Brahmins of Hindustan are like a fragrant soil
He who seen them cannot help falling in love

The hot sighs that are escaping from the mouth constantly
O Meer, it is clear they have burnt the heart already.

नागह[1] जो वह सनम[2] सितम-ईजाद[3] आ गया
देखे से तौर उसके खुदा याद आ गया

फोड़ा था सर तो हमने भी पर इसको क्या करें
जो चश्मे-रोज़गार[4] में फ़रहाद आ गया

अपना भी क़स्द[5] था सरे-दीवारे-बाग़ का
तोड़ा ही था क़फ़स[6] को कि सय्याद[7] आ गया

देखेंगे आदमी की रविश 'मीर' हम तेरी
गर सामने से टुक वो परीज़ाद[8] आ गया

Naagah jo weh sanam sitam-ijaad aa gaya
dekhe se taur uske khuda yaad aa gaya

Phora tha sar to humne bhi par isko kya karen
jo chashme-rozgaar mein Farhaad aa gaya

Apna bhi qasad tha sare-diware-baagh ka
tora hi tha qafas ko ki sayyad aa gaya

Dekhenge aadmi ki ravish 'Meer' hum teri
gar saamne se tuk woh parizaad aa gaya

---

1. अचानक 2. प्रियतम 3. निष्ठुर 4. दुनिया की आंख 5. इरादा 6. पिंजरा 7. चिड़ीमार 8. निष्ठुर-प्रेमी (प्रियतम)

If ever all of a sudden, my cruel beloved came
Seeing her ways, I remembered God's name

I too broke my head, but what could possibly be done
It's not me but Farhaad caught the world's ken

I was quite determined to fly off to the garden
But when I had just broken the cage open, came
the hunter and the game got undone

We will acknowledge your manhood O Meer, in case
My fairy-like beloved's charm you can face.

वो तुर्के-मस्त[1] किसू की खबर नहीं रखता
कि मैं शिकारे-ज़बूँ[2] हूँ, जिगर नहीं रखता

जिन्हों के दम में है तासीर और हैं वे लोग
हमारा नालाए-जांकाह[3] असर नहीं रखता

खुदा की ओर से यह एतबार है वरना
जो खूब देखो तो मैं कुछ हुनर नहीं रखता

जुदा जुदा फिरे है 'मीर' सब से किस खातिर
ख्याल मिलने का उसके अगर नहीं रखता

Woh turke-mast kisoo ki khabar nahin rakhta
ki main shikare-zaboon hoon jigar nahin rakhta

Jinhon ke dum mein hai taaseer aur hain ve log
humara naalaye-jaankaah asar nahin rakhta

Khuda ki ore se yeh aetbar hai verna
jo khoob dekho to main kuchh hunar nahin rakhta

Juda juda phire hai 'Meer' sab se kis khatir
khayal milne ka uske agar nahin rakhta

---

1. बेपरवाह प्रियतम 2. कमज़ोर शिकार 3. तीव्र रुदन

The cruel beloved cares for none
She considers not that hunting such a weak prey
as me is not much fun

Those whose words have effect are others, not I
There is no power to move even in my piercing cry

The confidence that I have is God-given
For if I look honestly for talent, I have none

If he is indifferent whether she meets him or not
Why is Meer with everybody so put off.

क्या कहें कुछ कहा नहीं जाता
अब तो चुप भी रहा नहीं जाता

ताक़ते-दिल तलक तअब[1] खैंचे
अब सितम तक सहा नहीं जाता

उस दुरे-तर[2] का हैराती[3] है बहर[4]
तब तो उससे बहा नहीं जाता

कब तेरी रह[5] में 'मीरे'-गर्द-आलूद[6]
लोहू में आ नहा नहीं जाता

Kya kahen kuchh kaha nahin jaata
ab to chup bhi raha nahin jaata

Taqte-dil talak taeb khenche
ab sitam tak saha nahin jaata

Us dure-tar ka hairaati hai behar
tab to usse baha nahin jaata

Kab teri reh mein 'Meere'-gard-aalood
lohu main aa naha nahine jaata

---

1. रंज 2. पानीदार मोती 3. प्रेम-मग्न 4. समुद्र 5. राह 6. धूलि-धूसरित 'मीर'

What shall I say, I just cannot speak, sir
But I am not able to keep quiet either

Sorrow is eating away all my strength
And even her cruelty I cannot bear

The ocean is caught in the love of that watery pearl
So it is stagnant and cannot stir

When was it that dust-besmeared Meer
Came and did not bathe in blood instead of water.

फ़िराक़[1] आंख लगने की जा[2] ही नहीं
पलक से पलक आशना[3] ही नहीं

मुहब्बत जहां की तहां हो चुकी
कुछ इस रोग की है दवा ही नहीं

वो क्या कुछ नहीं हुस्न के शहर में
नहीं है तो रस्मे-वफ़ा ही नहीं

नहीं दैर[4] अगर 'मीर' काबा तो है
हमारे कोई क्या खुदा ही नहीं

Firaq aankh lagne ki jaa hi nahin
palak se palak aashna hi nahin

Muhabbat jahaan ki tahaan ho chuki
kuchh is rog ki hai dawa hi nahin

Woh kya kuchh nahin husn ke shehar mein
nahin hai to rasme-wafa hi nahin

Nahin dair agar 'Meer' kaaba to hai
Humare koi kya khuda hi nahin

1. विरह 2. जगह 3. परिचित 4. मंदिर

O parting, the two eyelids just don't meet
Forget about slumber sweet

In this world love has become a fiction
There is no cure for this addiction

Except for faithfulness
Beauty has everything else

Do you think we have no God at all
If not temple we have Kaba tall.

वो आये बज़्म में इतना तो मीर ने देखा
फिर उसके बाद चिराग़ों में रोशनी न रही

शाम से ही बुझा-सा रहता है
दिल हुआ है चिराग़ मुफ़लिस का

आतिशे-इश्क़ ने रावण को जलाकर मारा
गर्चे लंका-का-सा था उस देव का सर पानी में

आंखें पथराई हैं छाती पत्थर है
वो ही जाने जो इन्तज़ार करे

हम मीर तेरा मरना क्या चाहते थे लेकिन
रहता है हुए बिन कब जो कुछ कि हुआ चाहे

→

Woh aaye bazm mein itna to Meer ne dekha
phir uske baad chiragon mein roshni na rahi

Shaam se hi bujha-sa rehta hai
dil hua hai chiraagh mufils ka

Aatishe-ishq ne ravan ko jalakar maara
garche lanka-ka-sa tha us dev ka sar paani mein

Aankhen pathrai hain chhati patthar hai
woh hi jaane jo intezaar kare

Hum Meer tera marna kya chahte the lekin
rehta hai hue bin kab jo kuchh ki hua chahe

Select Couplets

He came to the assembly, this much Meer could see
But after that the lamps lost their light instantly

Like a candle in a poor household
My heart, as the evening arrives, becomes dim and cold

Fires of love burnt even a wise man like Ravan into cinders
Although like Lanka, his head too was in water

Eyes are lifeless and the heart heavy
He alone knows who has to wait endlessly

O Meer, we didn't want you to die
But averting the inevitable did not in anybody's power lie

→

गर्चे उम्मीदे-असीरी[1] पे ये नाशाद आया
राम[2] सय्याद का होते ही ख़ुदा याद आया

दिल गया, रुसवा हुए, आख़िर को सौदा[3] हो गया
इस दो-रोज़ा-ज़ीस्त[4] में हम पर भी क्या-क्या हो गया

आने के वक़्त तुम तो कहीं के कहीं रहे
अब आये तुम तो फ़ायदा? हम ही नहीं रहे

नाचार हम तो तुझ बिन जी मार कर रहेंगे
पर इस रविश को तेरी यह लोग क्या कहेंगे

खाक से क्यों न 'मीर' यकसाँ[5] हूँ
मुझ पे तो आसमान टूटा है

→

Garche ummide-asiri pe ye nashaad aaya
Ram sayyad ka hote hi khuda yaad aaya

Dil gaya ruswa hue, aakhir ko sauda ho gaya
is do-roza-zist mein hum per bhi kya-kya ho gaya

Aane ke waqt tum to kahin ke kahin rahe
ab aaye tum to phayada? hum hi nahin rahe

Nachaar hum to tujh bin ji maar kar rahenge
par is ravish ko teri yeh log kya kahenge

Khaak se kyon na 'Meer' yaksaan hoon
mujh pe to aasmaan toota hai

1. कैद होने की आशा 2. वश में 3. उन्माद 4. दो दिन की ज़िन्दगी 5. मिला हुआ

Although the hopeless fellow came here to be encaged
As soon as he was in the clutches of the hunter, to the Almighty he prayed

I lost my heart, earned infamy and in the end went mad
O in a brief span of life how many misfortunes I have had

When my death was approaching, God know where had you been
It is no use coming now because now I am no longer to be seen

I, the helpless one will kill my desires and manage to live for a few days
But have you ever thought what the common man about your conduct after me says

Why shouldn't I be at level with the dust
The very heavens have on my head, burst

→

हम रो-रो के दर्दे-दिले-दीवाना कहेंगे
जी में है कभू हाले-ग़रीबाना कहेंगे

उम्र गुज़री कि तेरे कूचे में आने से गये
दूर से एक नज़र देख के जाने से गये

क्या कहूँ मैं 'मीर' अपनी सरगुज़िश्त[1]
इब्तदा[2] *क़िस्से ही में वह सो गया*

कूचाए-यार से न जावेंगे
कैसे ही होंगे हम गये गुज़रे

दिल ताब[3] *टुक भी लाता तो कहने में कुछ आता*
उस तिश्नाकाम[4] *ने तो पानी भी फिर न मांगा*

→

Hum ro-ro ke darde-dile-diwana kahenge
jee mein hai kabhu haale-gharibana kahenge

Umra guzri ki tere kuche ke aane se gaye
door se ek nazar dekh ke jaane se gaye

Kya kahoon main 'Meer' apni sarguzisht
ibtada kisse hi mein vah so gaya

Kuchaaye-yaar se na jaavenge
kaise hi honge hum gaye guzre

Dil taab tuk bhi laata to kehne mein kuchh aata
us tishnakaam ne to paani bhi phir na maanga

---

1. राम-कहानी 2. आरम्भ 3. सहन करने की शक्ति 4. प्यासा

My loud cries will express the agony of my heart
I have a mind to give tongue to my miserable lot

It is a long time now that I have not been to your street
Even from a distance for long I have not been able to see you

What do O Meer, of my experience I tell
Right in the beginning of the tale, in a slumber he fell

Even if I am a hopeless fellow
From my beloved's street, I will just not go

Only if it recovered a little, could the heart any word utter
But the poor thirsty creature had no strength even to ask for water

→

उन ने देखा जो उठ के सोते से
उड़ गये आइने के तोते से

देखता हूँ तो काम मेरा 'मीर'
अव्वले-इश्क़ ही में आखिर है

बस न लग चल नसीम[1] मुझ से कि मैं
रह गया हूँ चिराग़-सा बुझ कर

Un ne dekha jo uth ke sote se
ur gaye aaine ke tote se

Dekhta hoon to kaam mera 'Meer'
awwale-ishq hi mein aakhir hai

Bus na lag chal naseem mujh se ki main
reh gaya hoon chiraag se bujh kar

1. सुबह की हवा

As she woke up and saw her face in the mirror
The poor mirror felt small as it saw her glamour

In the beginning of my love itself, as I see
O Meer, my work is complete

Bother me not O breeze, prithee
I am a candle burnt out already.

एक मसनवी

चमन से इनायत के बादाम दार
इलाही ज़बां दे मुझे मग्ज़दार

सिफ़त इश्क़ की ता[1] करूं मैं बयां
रहूं इश्क़ कहने से मैं तर ज़बां

अजब इश्क़ है मर्दे-कार-आमदा[2]
जहां दोनों इसके हैं बरहमज़दा[3]

जहां जंग सफ़[4] की ये ज़ालिम लड़ा
सफ़ उलटी, जहां एक मारा पड़ा

अगर लोग मारे गये सर-बसर
हुई फ़तह उसकी ये है तुरफ़ातर[5]

कोई कुश्तनी[6] जो तरफ़[7] हो गया
तहे-तेग़[8] उसके तलफ़[9] हो गया

→

Chaman se inayat ke badaam daar
ilaahi zabaan de mujhe magzdaar

Siphat ishq ki taa karun main bayaan
rahoon ishq kahne se main tar zabaan

Ajab ishq hai marde-kaar-aamda
jahan donon iske hain berhumzada

Jahan jung saf ki ye zaalim lara
saf ulti jahan ek maara para

Agar log maare gaye sar-basar
hui fateh uski ye hai turfaatar

Koi kushtani jo taraf ho gaya
tahe-tegh uske talaf ho gaya

---

1. ताकि 2. युद्ध-वीर 3. बरबाद किये हुए 4. सैनिक पंक्ति 5. विशेष बात 6. मरने माला 7. आकृष्ट 8. तलवार के नीचे 9. नष्ट

Masnavi (A love Poem)

Like the almond tree to the garden
O God, give a tongue effective

So that I can sing a song in praise of love
And am in proper frame of mind to tell my tale

Love is a strange warrior
That destroys both the lovers;

Where ever this cruel love rules
The whole scheme goes awry and everybody is annihilated;
If everybody is by it killed
Then it is a fallacy to call anybody victorious.

If a person is bewitched by love
He is sure to be ruined,

→

जहां जिस किसू से इसे चाह है
वहीं उसके ता-क़त्ल[1] हमराह है

किसू से अगर हो गयी लाग सी
दरूनी[2] में उसके लगी आग सी

हुआ मुल्तफ़ित यह किसू पर कहीं
तो नामो-निशां उसका फिर वां नहीं

वफ़ाक़[3] इसका निकला सरासर निफ़ाक़[4]
पड़ा आशिक़ों में अजब इत्तफ़ाक़

जवां कैसे-कैसे मुए इश्क़ में
बहुत घर खराबे[5] हुए इश्क़ में

बहुत इश्क़ में लोग रोगी हुए
बहुत खाक मल मुँह पे जोगी हुए

→

Jahan jis kisu se ise chaah hai
wahin uske taa-qatl humraah hai

Kisu se agar ho gayee laag si
daruni mein uske lagi aag si

Hua multafit yeh kisu per kahin
to naamo-nishan uska phir waan nahin

Wafaaq iska nikla sarasar nifaaq
para aashiqon mein ajab ittefaaq

Jawan kaise-kaise mue ishq mein
bahut ghar kharabe hue ishq mein

Bahut ishq mein log rogi hue
bahut khaak mal munh pe jogi hue

---

1. कत्ल होने तक 2. दिल 3. दोस्ती 4. दुश्मनी 5. खंडहर

It is an abiding passion
Once you come under its sway

A fire burns in your heart
And it leaves you not till your death

Once it takes hold of somebody
Not a trace of him will be ultimately found

Its friendship is no better than enmity—
This is the common thread binding all lovers

Many a promising youth has been undone by it
And many a household destroyed

Innumerable people have fallen prey to it
And so many have become mendicants;

→

गये दश्त[1] में कुछ नमद-मू[2] हुए
कुछ इक शहर में फिरके यकसू हुए

न मुर्ग़े-चमन ही है नालां-ओ-ज़ार[3]
गये दाग़ कुहसार[4] से लालाज़ार[5]

किसू का जिगर ग़म से ख़ूं हो गया
किसू कोहकन[6] को जुनूं हो गया

कोई ज़ार[7] बारां[8] बहुत रो चुका
कोई बर्क़[9] सा जल-बुझा हो चुका

ग़रज़ इश्क़ का हर तरफ़ ज़ोर है
नयी रोज़ शहरों में एक गोर[10] है

बहुत जान नाकाम देते गये
तमन्नाए-दिल साथ लेते गये

→

Gaye dasht mein kuchh namad-mu hue
kuchh ik shehar mein phirke yaksu hue

Na murge-chaman hi hai nalaan-o-zaar
gaye daagh kuhsaar se laalazaar

Kisu ka jigar ghum se khoon ho gaya
kisu kohkan ko junoon ho gaya

Koi zaar baraan bahut ro chuka
koi burq sa jal-bujha ho chuka

Garaz ishq ka har taraf zor hai
nayi roz shahron mein ik gor hai

Bahut jaan nakaam dete gaye
tamannye-dil saath lete gaye

---

1. जंगल 2. बाल बिखराये 3. दुखी और रोते हुए 4. पहाड़ 5. गुले-लाला के जंगल 6. पहाड़ काटने वाला (फ़रहाद) 7. दुखी 8. वर्षा 9. बिजली 10. कब्र

Many took to the forest in a dishevelled state
While some wandered alone about town;

The garden is denuded of its flowers
And no one grieves for them.

Someone's heart is rent apart
Some mountain-cutter went insane

Some miserable fellow has cried no end
While another is like the lightning come and gone—

In short, love is on the rampage everywhere
And new graves come up every day.

Many a miserable lover laid down his life
And took his unfulfilled desire to the grave.

→

बहुत अहले-इस्लाम काफ़िर हुए
बहुत अव्वले-इश्क़ आख़िर हुए

बहुत जुर्मे-उल्फ़त पे मारे गये
जुआ इश्क़ का खेले, हारे गये

हुए खान्दां कैसे-कैसे खराब
जवां ज्यूं जवानी गये क्या शिताब[1]

किया इश्क़ जिस दिन से, मरते रहे
जियों ही का अंदेशा करते रहे

किसे इश्क़ ने जी से मारा नहीं
यही दर्द है जिसका चारा[2] नहीं

→

Bahut ahle-islaam kaafir hue
bahut awwale-ishq aakhir hue

Bahut jurme-ulphat pe maare gaye
jua ishq ka khele, haare gaye

Hue khandaan kaise-kaise kharaab
jawan jyun jawani gaye kya shitaab

Kiya ishq jis din se marte rahe
jiyon hi ka andesha karte rahe

Kise ishq ne jee se maara nahin
yahi dard hai jiska chaara nahin

1. जल्दी 2. इलाज

Many a believer in Islam has become infidel
And many right in the beginning of the affair
ceased to be

Many a one lost the game of love
And has been most severely punished for this crime;

Many a cheerful youth came to grief
And prematurely bade good-bye

And always apprehensive about his life
The day he fell in love, he began to die.

Who in love has not lost his heart!
This is one malady which has no cure,

→

जो हो इश्क़ आरिज़[1] तो फिर यास[2] है
अबस[3] कोई दिन जीने का पास[4] है

मुहब्बत है नैरंग-साज़े-अजीब[5]
फ़साने हैं उसके अजीबो-ग़रीब

कहीं इश्क़ से आरज़ू-कुश[6] गये
गये खुश जो आशिक़ सो नाखुश गये

कहीं काम इसने किये हैं अजब
फ़साना हुई बज़्मे-ऐशो-तरब[7]

कहीं बादशाह इस से दरवेश हैं
कहीं इससे दरवेश दिलरेश[8] हैं

→

Jo ho ishq aariz to phir yaas hai
abus koi din jeene ka paas hai

Muhabbat hai nairang-saaze-ajeeb
phasane hain uske ajeebo-ghareeb

Kahin ishq se aarzoo-kush gaye
gaye khush jo aashiq so nakhush gaye

Kahin kaam isne kiye hain ajab
phasana hui bazme-aesho-tarab

Kahin baadshah isse darvesh hain
kahin isse darvesh dilresh hain

1. आवश्यक 2. निराशा 3. बेकार 4. ख़याल 5. जादूगर 6. इच्छाओं का खून करने वाला 7. खुशी की महफ़िल 8. दुखी

If you cannot help falling in love
Disapointment is your lot;

Love is a strange magician
And equally strange are its tales.

The lovers who started in joy, ended in pain
And some time a hardy one came to grief;

Strange are its deeds, indeed.
Some where a happy assembly became a tale,

Because of it, some king became a faqir
While some mendicants are mauld by it;

→

लिया काह[1] का कोह[2] से कीं[3] कहीं
मिलाये कहीं आसमानो-ज़मीं

कहीं पड़ गये इसे फ़ितने फ़साद
रहे ज़ेरे-शमशीर[4] हद से ज़ियाद

हुए इश्क़ में ज़हद-केशां[5] खराब
रहे दिल शिकस्ता परीशां खराब

मुसलमां हुए इश्क़ में बरहमन
गये काबे को छोड़ दीने-कुहन[6]

न सबहा[7] न ज़ुन्नार[8] नै कुफ्रो-दीं
जहाँ सब है इश्क़ और कुछ भी नहीं

मुहब्बत के सागर-कश[9] अहले-सलाह[10]
ये बेहोश दारू हैं इनकी फ़लाह[11]

→

Liya kah ka koh se kin kahin
milaye kahin aasmaano-zameen

Kahin par gaye ise phitne fasaad
rahe zere-shamsheer hud se ziyaad

Hue ishq mein zehad-keshaan kharaab
rahe dil shikasta parishan kharaab

Musalman hue ishq mein berhuman
gaye kaabe to chhor deene-kuhan

Na sabaha na zunnar na kufro-deen
jahan sab hai ishq aur kuchh bhi nahin

Muhabbat ke sagar-kash ahle-salaah
ye behosh daaroo hain inkei falaah

---

1. घास 2. पहाड़ 3. बैर 4. तलवार तले 5. कर्मकांडी 6. पुराना धर्म 7. माला 8. जनेऊ 9. शराबी 10. परहेज़गार 11. बेहतरी

Sometime the humble grass gets pitted against a
mighty mountain
And sometime this love does a miracle unimaginable.

Sometime this love creates riots
And hangs like the sword of Domocles on so many
heads.

Many a ritual-loving pious man has gone astray
And roams bewildered and heart-broken;

So many Muslims have left Kaba and their religion
And have become Brahmins

But not taking to either rosary or the sacred thread
Because in their world, there is nothing but love.

In love, even the most abstentious ones have become
hard drinkers;
No lover in his senses remains.

→

यही इश्क़ जिससे कि हासिल है काम
यही इश्क़ है जिससे निकला है नाम

इसी इश्क़ से रू-सियह[1] रू-सफ़ेद[2]
रखें इश्क़ से ना-उमेदां उमेद

यही इश्क़ है अक्दए-दिल[3] है यह
यही इश्क़ हल्लाले-मुश्किल[4] है यह

Yahi ishq jisse ki haasil hai kaam
yahi ishq hai jisse nikla hai naam

Isee ishq se ru-siyah ru-saphed
rakhen ishq se naa-umedan umed

Yahi ishq hai aqdaye-dil hai yeh
yahi ishq hallaale mushkil hai yeh

---

1. बदनाम 2. नेकनाम 3. दिल की गांठ 4. मुश्किल हल करने वाला

Notwithstanding all the mayhem caused by it,
however
Love is not entirely a curse.

Because of it, some people become famous or
notorious
It creates both despondency and hope

This love can be heart-sore
As also it solves all your problems.

यारों को कदूरतें[1] हैं अब तो हम से
जिस रोज़ कि हम जायेंगे आलम से
उस रोज़ खुलेगा साफ़ उन पर ये राज़
इस बज़्म में रौनक थी हमारे दम से

Yaaron ko kaduraten hain ab to hum se
jis roz ki hum jayenge aalam se
Us roz khulega saaf un per ye raaz
is bazm mein raunak thi humare dum se

1. शत्रुता

A quartrain

Now my friends are hostile to me
But the day I die, they will be sorry
They will realize that it was because me only
That there was life the assembly

रुबाइयां

हर रोज़ नया एक तमाशा देखा
हर कूचे सौ जवाने रअना[1] देखा
दिल्ली थी तिलिस्मात कि हर जगह मीर
इन आंखों से हमने वाह क्या-क्या देखा

Har roz naya ek tamasha dekha
har kuche sau jawane-raena dekha
dilli thi tilismaat ki har jagah Meer
in aankhon se humane waah kya-kya dekha

1. खूबसूरत जवान

A quartrain

I witnessed a new fair every day
There were handsome youngmen in every street
Delhi was a marvellous city where everywhere
In every eye there was a dream strange and sweet.

❑❑❑